Creative Pricing

Contributors

Morton Backer

Jules Backman

R. Granger Benson

Leigh Carter

Edward W. Cundiff

Robert E. Good

Douglas P. Gould

Sherman P. Haight, Jr.

J. Sidney Johnson

Michael J. Loftus

Alfred R. Oxenfeldt

Gordon T. Roberts

Richard C. Sarset

Robert E. Sibson

Peter G. Scotese

Richard J. Steele

Fred M. Truett

Donald B. Tuson

Otto Wheeley

CREATIVE PRICING

edited by

Elizabeth Marting

American Management Association

Foreword

PERHAPS THE ONE STATEMENT TO WHICH THE 19 CONTRIBUTING AUTHORS represented in this book would subscribe without hesitation is that pricing is a function which directly affects corporate profits and therefore deserves management attention at the very highest levels. Perhaps, too, they would agree that no other management function, improperly handled, can so tarnish the company's image in the eyes of the buying public and even, in extreme cases, the public at large.

Certainly pricing policy is so much a part of the company's overall philosophy, ethical position, and way of life that it is inescapably a top management responsibility. Moreover, the innumerable factors which must be considered—plus the quantities of data essential to day-by-day price administration—demand that the decision makers have sufficient status in the organization to marshal the data and sufficient breadth of knowledge to take all the factors, both economic and uneconomic, into account. Their decisions will affect the company no matter what their skill, no matter how honest their motives or how great their reverence for free enterprise—in pricing as in every phase of marketing a product or a service. It is the thesis of this book that with sound planning, flexible techniques, and adequate support, pricing can be made to have a positive, productive impact on company profits; in short, that it can be *creative*.

The authors, considered individually, have given this controversial area of management responsibility much thought. Some of them have made it a specialty. Their combined backgrounds range over a broad variety of situations and problems: large companies and small ones, industrial goods and consumer goods, established product lines and innovations, retailers and wholesalers. The thinking of the theorist is balanced by the experience of the practical executive. We are grateful for the forthrightness with which all of them have approached a difficult subject.

Collectively, these authors reflect a serious concern with pricing policy and methods on the part of business and industry as a whole. This concern is vital and, therefore, healthy. Dr. Backman begins his concluding chapter by reminding us that the environment in which pricing decisions are being made has changed markedly in the past quarter-century: competitive pressures have intensified, the public relations and "respectability" aspects of pricing are more and more important, and government is extending its influence through legislation, the activities of federal agencies, and the rulings of the courts. Yet Dr. Backman is merely driving home the point made over and over in earlier chapters by his fellow contributors. They leave no doubt that those charged with pricing policy and administration are alert to this changing environment and are seeking consciously to meet its requirements.

No one can be a price leader every time; there must inevitably, as these pages demonstrate, be both leaders and followers. Both should find here guides to truly constructive, creative pricing.

—E.M.

Contents

Introduction:
The Role of Price
and Pricing Reconsidered

Alfred R. Oxenfeldt

THE NOTION THAT PRICING CAN BE CREATIVE IS ITSELF QUITE CREATIVE AND new. For centuries, price setters considered only a few quite obvious alternatives: keep prices where they are, raise or lower them, and sell now or hold for future sale.

Business executives today have many choices. For example, they can—and ordinarily would be well advised to—combine changes in price with shifts in advertising, personal sales efforts, promotional activities, special efforts with marketing channels, shifts in service, changed credit terms, and the like. Also, they can change certain prices while keeping others constant, raising some while reducing others—or changing some by large amounts and others by a little. Similarly, they can change prices at this time rather than that.

DR. OXENFELDT is Professor of Marketing in Columbia University's Graduate School of Business.

9

Apart from such alternatives, moreover, price setters enjoy wide choice with respect to the content of price-related actions. In their advertising, they may excuse or capitalize on their price changes in a great variety of ways. And they may associate price changes with many possible variations in product, if only in superficial appearance or package. The numerous variables controllable by the price setter offer him an opportunity to create wholly new combinations of marketing actions, of which price changes form a part.

The statement that price setters have the opportunity to be creative runs counter to the writing and thinking of most economic theorists. If they misunderstand the pricing functions of present-day business executives, economists probably also misunderstand the role played by price in the operation of our economy. Accordingly, the first subject we shall discuss here is that role. Thereupon, we shall explore the place of pricing in the success of individual firms. These questions are not unrelated—for, if business success comes largely at the expense of the economy, the rules of the game are likely to be changed to eliminate the conflict between private and social gain.

Price in a Modern Industrial Economy

Why do so many people believe that a price system will allocate productive resources and ration output efficiently? What is a price system? How is it said to work? What are the basic mechanisms that it incorporates? When do they function well and when poorly?

RATIONALE FOR THE CASE THAT A PRICE SYSTEM WILL BE HIGHLY EFFICIENT

When most people speak about a price system, they ordinarily have in mind at least four quite separate notions: first, that buyers and sellers are in direct and active competition with one another; second, that there should be a condition of free enterprise (that is, individuals should possess the right to engage in any line of business activity); third, persons engaged in business should be motivated primarily by monetary gain; and, fourth, there should be a *free system of prices* for labor, land, instruments of production, liquid funds, and so on and for the output of commercial enterprises. The term "price system" often is used to refer only to the fourth of these notions. Prices are employed as an economic tool by centrally planned economies as well as by so-called capitalist economies, but they do not usually provide for vigorous competition, free enterprise, and the profit motive.

Let us first consider the interconnection among the four elements ordinarily considered features of a price system. Vigorous competition is not an inevitable result either of free enterprise or of the profit system. In part, vigorous competition requires a willingness to—indeed, the taking of pleasure in—injuring one's rivals. (It surprises many American businessmen to learn that businessmen in many other countries shrink from the destructive side of competitive behavior.) Also, free enterprise may be limited by such means as licensing requirements, but competition may be keen among those who hold licenses. Similarly, the striving for monetary gain is not equally strong among individuals or nations, whether or not they have free enterprise or keen competition.

Where a free price system is combined with vigorous competition, free enterprise, and the profit motive, one would expect a highly efficient economic system for the following reasons: First, in such an economy, individuals—both as sellers of their services and as buyers of products—make economic decisions that affect them directly and immediately. Accordingly, the matters they decide are those about which they know most. (Contrast this with their expressions of opinion about foreign policy or the appropriate size of the national debt.) Moreover, their decisions are markedly decentralized and limited in scope. If a small minority makes errors, these presumably are canceled to a considerable degree by errors in the opposite direction by others; consequently, the net effect of their errors is only minor. In contrast, if the decisions of certain individuals—say, economic planners—affected broad sectors of industry, their errors would do serious harm.

It is argued that a price system (combined with free enterprise, vigorous competition, and a profit system) incorporates a delicately calibrated system of penalties and rewards. Such a price system records the preferences of individuals—with respect to both employment and products. It also creates pressures within the economy to honor those preferences. Specifically, a price system allows individuals to express fine shades of preference for alternative products. They do so by the prices they offer for them; the greater their desire for a product, for example, the more they will offer for it. Since prices can vary by tiny amounts, individuals can express quite precisely the degree of their desire.

Individuals seeking employment (and owners of private or liquid funds) indicate how much they dislike alternative employment and unemployment by the amount of compensation they demand. The wage and salary demands of prospective employees reflect both what they can earn in alternative employment and their evaluation of the nonmonetary aspects of each possibility. The price system thus permits individuals to express delicate shadings of desire and distaste.

When products bear a high price, consumers have a strong incentive to find alternatives that offer them greater satisfaction per dollar. High price penalizes a buyer; since price can vary by tiny amounts, it can discourage purchase in the desired degree. In this way, the prices of different goods can stand in such a relationship to one another that they encourage the use of those that involve low sacrifices in production for members of the economy while discouraging the use of products whose production involves heavy sacrifices.

Businessmen are likewise under pressure to keep their penalties (costs) to a minimum; that is, they are penalized heavily when they use scarce resources, and they reduce their penalties when they economize in the use of productive resources. Ideally, a price system fixes penalties on the use of products and production factors that create precisely the desired pressure on potential users to economize in their use. Moreover, an ideal price system is characterized by very flexible prices for finished output, wages, salaries, interest, rent, royalties, and the like that reflect *changes* in the valuations made by buyers of goods and sellers of services. And these variations in prices, wages, and so on are claimed to be of precisely the amount required to obtain the desired degree of use and of substitution.

In the ideal price system we hypothesize, resources would flow quickly to occupations where profits are highest. The strong profit motive we assume would insure this result. Consequently, the output of products in short supply would be expanded promptly, and high profits would prevail only briefly. Thus high profit rates would perform the vital economic function of attracting resources to those places where output is deficient; conversely, low profits and losses would repel resources as well as prod existing productive factors to leave those sectors of the economy where output is excessive.

FUNCTIONS ATTRIBUTED TO PRICES

The foregoing rationale for a price system attributes a variety of functions to prices. Let us single out the more important of these for examination.

First, prices of output are asserted to have particular effects upon the level of output; specifically, high prices (relative to costs) raise output, and low prices tend to reduce it. Similarly, wage rates are asserted to influence the supply of labor offered to employers in a favorable way—bringing workers to places where their services are needed and hastening their exit where they exist in excessive numbers. Similarly, relative prices are credited with influencing the proportions in which buyers and producers purchase items when they have substitutes available.

Do prices actually work in the manner assumed? To answer this question, we must understand why prices are said to perform the functions attributed to them. In other words, how do price changes influence output, the proportions in which goods are purchased, employment, and so forth? Moreover, what changes in the economy will give rise to price changes, and how promptly will they occur? Are the responses of participants in the economy to price changes as described in our rationale?

Two main functions that are attributed to prices account for the great power they are said to exert: First, they *provide "signals"* to participants in business activity; second, they *motivate participants* in the economy. We shall take a quick look at each of these functions both to understand better what is assumed and to assess the validity of these assumptions. It need scarcely be stated that the subjects raised are very complex and the treatment they are given here is sketchy. However, we shall carry our discussion far enough to suggest some of the reasons for the high regard in which many hold the price system and for the doubts of its opponents.

1. *Prices as a signaling system.* Perhaps the most important function attributed to prices is that of providing signals that call attention to the "need" for change and thus trigger desired economic action. What kinds of desired action in the economy are signaled by prices, to whom are these signals given, how clear and prompt are these signals, and do they produce the desired results?

In the preceding sketch of a price system, prices were said to provide signals that increases or reductions in output are needed. More specifically, prices were said to rise, when demands for products increase, and thus signal the need for more output. It was suggested that a rise in price would both attract newcomers to a trade and encourage existing firms to expand output. Let us see how price works as a signal in this case, assuming that increased desire for output on the part of buyers does, in fact, lead to a rise in price.

It would rarely be an increase in price that would initially lead established firms to increase output; rather, it would be either a rise in orders (which presumably could be filled at a profit) or a rise in anticipated profitability. Presumably, the price increase would be a signal to potential entrants into the industry only if it were taken as evidence that profit opportunities had risen for producers of the item in question.

But do higher prices signify higher profits? Sometimes they do, surely. On frequent occasions, however, they do not at all. Not infrequently, costs rise and force prices up; the price rise may be smaller than the cost increase, thus depressing profit margins. And, at the higher prices, usually less is sold, thus forcing total profits down. Under these circumstances—not uncommon ones—a rise in price will signal a reduction in profitability. *In other words, prices are, at best, an indirect and unreliable indicator of profit opportunities.* To obtain the desired results, businessmen require prompt signals of profit opportunities, and these are sorely lacking in a real-life free enterprise economy—though they are assumed implicitly in much that is written about the workings of a price system.

It should also be observed that established firms have available to them a reliable and prompt signal of a change in demand in the form of varying orders. Orders give fairly precise indications of the magnitude of the demand increase, whereas *it would be difficult to draw direct inferences from any given price increase to the amount by which demand had increased.* In short, prices are quite ambiguous signals—at least of changes in demand—and they may not even be needed. Potential entrants could observe changes in sales and output by established firms almost as easily as changes in their price; indeed, in many trades, increased sales precede changes in price by a considerable period when demand increases. Usually the first price signal of a drop in demand is a rise in the number of sales that a firm makes off list price—a signal available only to itself. Conversely, this number will fall and possibly become zero when demand rises—but the signal will not be visible to persons outside the firm.

Signals of a need for changes in output because of changed demand clearly would be valuable in any economy. Such signals should be unambiguous and prompt if they are to avoid delay or unnecessary shortages or overexpansion. One would judge from general industry practice that firms do not, in fact, use prices as indicators of the need to expand output. Much more often, they use the results of marketing research and general sales forecasting techniques—especially when expansion of plant and equipment is involved.

These few paragraphs hardly represent an exhaustive analysis of the nature and effectiveness of prices as signaling devices. They should, however, sharpen some key issues and raise serious questions about reliance upon prices to perform that function.

2. Prices as a motivating device. It has already been indicated that prospective profit, rather than price, motivates most business decisions and that price changes do perform some useful functions related to motivation; that should not pass unmentioned.

First, prices are much more public—though far from being entirely so—than profits and profit margins. Second, they change more sharply and visibly than actual profits, which respond only after a time lag. As a result, prices do help to inform outsiders to a trade that changes in potential profits may be taking place. As such, they are potentially valuable signals.

These signals are referred to here in connection with motivation because the price change does alter the financial terms of transactions. Consequently, they almost certainly will be accompanied by some change in profitability—though not necessarily by changes in the same direction or proportion. Taken by themselves, higher prices can lead to the hope that profit prospects have improved and, if the outsider knows nothing else, may be so interpreted. In a set of circumstances whereby a price change is accompanied by an assumption that costs and unit sales have not changed correspondingly, one may find a *motive* for a change in behavior.

How the U.S. Economy Differs from an Idealized Price System

Discussions of the price system and of markets in general usually are characterized by great optimism, if not wishful thinking. As John K. Galbraith has recently stated, "to them [classical economists] the market is more than an institution. It is a mystique, a supernatural endowment which evokes not technical, but religious, attitudes." [1]

---

[1] Reported in *The New York Times* Book Review Section, June 25, 1967, p. 3.

This worship of a price system clearly stems from economic writings, and these find their origins in economic thought at a time when economic systems were totally unlike those of the present day. At that time, most economic enterprises were producing "commodities" rather than brands of a product; in the absence of brand identification, customers had no reason to select among vendors in the same market on grounds other than price. The present world of sophisticated advertising (designed to create favorable brand images and build customer loyalty), frequent product modifications, the offering of valuable and complex customer services, the dependence of producers upon resellers for market exposure, and the like is a far cry from conditions in France and England in the late 1700's and early 1800's. One might term certain sectors of the U.S. economy "advertising systems," "personal selling systems," or "product change systems" quite as much as "price systems."

Moreover, the U.S. economy is clearly pluralistic,[2] representing a combination of highly dissimilar sectors in which prices and profits have a very different significance. Major economic activities are operated directly by the government at the federal, state, and local levels; by nonprofit organizations (hospitals, higher educational institutions, cultural institutions, foundation-supported research activity); and by private businesses which sell almost exclusively to government and are therefore heavily, albeit indirectly, controlled by government.

Having said all this, we might content ourselves with lamenting the deplorable state of our understanding of modern markets and let matters rest there. Or we might go further and explain what needs to be known if one is to understand the role of prices and the nature of modern markets and perhaps indicate the kinds of research that would enable us to know and understand them better. But the sticky question remains: What do we know about the role of price in our economy? Before we tackle this difficult question, we can state some general conclusions that may clear the ground and reduce confusion.

1. The role of price—its importance, its functioning, its effects on such matters as the flow of resources and the efficiency of production and distribution—varies widely from one industrial sector to another. Even within the free enterprise sector, price possibly var-

---

2 See Ginzberg, E., D. Hiestand, and B. Reubens, *The Pluralistic Economy,* McGraw-Hill Book Company, New York, 1965.

ies almost as much in significance as it does among different sectors.

2. Even within a single industry or market, the importance of price to the success of an individual firm differs widely; some firms base their appeal for patronage upon low price while others use a high-price appeal, for example.

3. In some industries, sellers enjoy considerable latitude as to the choice of price; that is, they can obtain tolerable amounts of patronage at a variety of prices. In other industries, sellers have almost no discretion with respect to price. If they do not conform very closely to the prevailing price in the market, they will obtain almost no business.

Consequently, generalizations about price cannot apply very widely. Indeed, only this generalization about price has a high degree of validity.

What questions shall we try to answer about the role of price in the U.S. economy? Shall we take the viewpoint of the economic theorist who wishes to explain the allocation of resources among alternative opportunities for employment? Or should we assume the viewpoint of a participant—a buyer or a seller? Should we perhaps adopt the viewpoint of a government representative who is concerned mainly with public welfare?

Further, do we wish to *describe* how markets operate—and in particular how they respond to changes in price? Or is our purpose to *explain* why markets operate as they do? Or would we *prescribe* behavior for businessmen or customers or for government? Possibly, we want to *evaluate* market phenomena from either a private or a social viewpoint. The many choices of viewpoint and purpose open to us can be presented in the form of a matrix (Exhibit 1).

It would be helpful to recognize that most writings about the market mechanism and the role of price in our economy have adopted the viewpoint of the economist and have sought to explain and evaluate market phenomena (Exhibit 1, cells 5 and 14). Although intended for other purposes, these writings have been used as the basis for general predictive and prescriptive statements and are presumed, by many, to hold for both businessmen and makers of public policy. One cannot emphasize too strongly that much of the literature discussing the functioning of markets is inappropriate for such uses. Price theory and market theory represent a body of very simple models intended to serve quite different purposes. To de-

EXHIBIT 1

ALTERNATIVE VIEWPOINTS
FOR ASSESSING THE ROLE OF PRICE IN THE ECONOMY

Point of View			
Purpose	Business Executive	Economist	Maker of Public Policy
Describe	1	2	3
Explain	4	5	6
Predict	7	8	9
Prescribe	10	11	12
Evaluate	13	14	15

scribe, explain, prescribe, predict, or evaluate real-life market situations in their full complexity, one must extend these models greatly to include many factors that they hold constant—and, for all practical purposes, actually ignore.

To explain the role of price in the present U.S. economy so that business executives can do their jobs better, we must make maximum use of what we know empirically about markets and, in addition, ask some fairly straightforward questions which may not even have been raised. We seek no universal generalizations; probabilistic statements will serve us nicely. Our main goal is to explain how prices affect the economy and to suggest their significance to business executives and others.

How Prices Operate in Typical Modern Industrial Markets

As has already been stated frequently, markets and industrial sectors in the free enterprise of the economy differ markedly. We cannot hope to discuss them all. Instead, we will concentrate our discussion on one type of market. Once this type is examined in depth, it will be possible to adjust what is said to take into account major differences between it and other types of market. (We use the term "market" quite loosely at this point;

little violence would be done if one thought of the term as synonymous with "industry.") The circumstances that we are assuming are:

1. A moderate number of firms make similar—though not identical —product-service offerings.
2. Some of these firms are substantially larger—and not necessarily more efficient—than others.
3. The firms in any industry vary widely in profitability, and rate of profit on investment or sales does not correlate closely with size.
4. Firms vary in rate of growth, in the number of related and unrelated items that they produce, in the number of geographic markets they cultivate, and in the kinds of customers they seek to attract.
5. Firms also vary in resources (financial and personal), strategies, constraints, and objectives.
6. The actions (whether wise or unwise) of any firm in the market will affect the rest very differently. Some will be strongly, quickly, and directly affected; others will be barely affected at all.
7. The validity with which rivals perceive and interpret the motives and impact of another firm's actions varies considerably.
8. Some sellers enjoy considerable customer loyalty; that is, they obtain a high proportion of repeat business.
9. Important differences exist among the managements of individual firms in their desire to increase profits, expand sales, and "make a showing" for the board of directors.

To what extent are such industries governed by prices? This general question is too loose and vague to permit an answer. It is clear that prices affect many aspects of businessmen's behavior and decisions. Our interest is in whether and to what extent other factors beyond price exert a significant influence. To be more specific, we are concerned with the following questions:

1. What factors determine who and how many firms will enter an industry? More specifically, to what extent is price governing, and to what extent do other factors determine the nature of entry?
2. What factors determine whether, when, and to what extent estab-

lished firms expand their facilities? Again, how important are nonprice factors?

3. What are the main determinants of the total quantity of any product that is purchased by customers? To what extent is the total demand influenced by nonprice factors?

4. What factors determine which sellers will be patronized most heavily by customers? To what extent is patronage dictated by nonprice factors?

5. What factors determine the kinds of products that are offered to consumers? To what extent are they dictated by price-profit considerations alone?

No easy answers exist for these questions, and one must not expect broad generalizations that apply to all industries. However, a simple inspection of these questions suggests that price is only one of many forces operating and not always the most important one. As a case in point, we realize that many actions taken by business are dictated by their basic strategy rather than by short-term profit analysis. For example, strategies related to growth, to size, and to complexion of product line exert strong influences on the number and types of firms that enter industries.

Similarly, many factors beyond price determine the total quantity of goods that customers will purchase. The total size of any market depends heavily upon the breadth of its exposure to potential buyers, the amount of advertising support it receives, the imaginativeness of promotions developed to spur sales, and the like. Sales of a product can be changed substantially, and price is not always the most important influence on total volume.

Moreover, the notion that firms will stay out of markets where the average rate of profit is low is highly suspect. Not infrequently, a new firm can make a profitable place for itself by pushing aside weak members of an industry. It is not prevailing prices or profits that matter, but the prices and profits that will accrue to the newcomer. So long as business managements take an aggressive view and are prepared to seek positions in markets by displacing other firms, the role of prevailing price and profit becomes relatively less important.

These arguments admittedly do not answer the five questions posed earlier. Nevertheless, they should suggest that price is not the prime mover in the present economy. Perhaps the modest importance of price in many industries is implicit in the following statement, which is heard often and in many versions: "I do not much care what price I pay for that item as long as no other firm can buy it for less than I pay." In the case of the ultimate consumer, he routinely buys—and seems to prefer—brands that are not the very lowest in price.

Price for the Individual Firm

So much, then, for the role of price in a modern economy. Let us now discuss the role of price from the standpoint of an individual firm. More specifically, we shall consider a few aspects of price that have gone largely undiscussed in the literature. A consideration of some of these issues will suggest the opportunity to exercise creativity in pricing. Again, the following pages only sketch a difficult subject, but they will, it is to be hoped, establish that price setting need be no dull and routine activity.

Before considering these neglected aspects of price, however, let us try to identify the situations in which pricing skill contributes heavily to the success of a firm and when it is relatively unimportant.

The Role of Price in the Success of a Firm

Does skill in pricing contribute much to the success of many executives and their firms? We rarely hear of managers who are outstanding because they excel in setting price; indeed, we know little about the participation of the nation's top business leaders in pricing. Further, we cannot tell with any confidence, even after the fact, whether most price decisions were "right," "wise," or "well advised." It appears that outsiders can rate the skill and effectiveness of a firm's advertising efforts, sales force, distributors, services, product, and packaging with considerable confidence. Apparently this is not the case with price.

Some executives undoubtedly are far more skillful in setting price than others, and their skill must affect their firms' profitability. However, it appears impossible to take the profit performance of a firm and account for it by the various ingredients required to operate a business successfully. Although one hears much about attempts to measure the effectiveness of advertising, we hear nothing about measuring the effectiveness of pricing.

What factors explain the importance of pricing skill in the success of a firm? It is likely that two dominate: the degree of a price setter's discretion over price and the size of the firm's net profits on sales. If any deviation from the prevailing price by the firm would involve an intolerable drop in sales, clearly no particular skill will be required to set price. Conversely, the price setter will exercise considerable discretion if his firm can perform reasonably well at a variety of prices (though not equally well); he may be able to improve the firm's profits very substantially in this way.

Accordingly, to explain the importance of pricing skill in business success, we must explain the degree of discretion possessed by the price setter. This we do in the matrix shown as Exhibit 2, which attributes different degrees of price discretion to two factors: similarity of sellers' offerings and customer concern with price. It suggests that price discretion is greatest when offerings are highly dissimilar and when customers are mainly concerned with nonprice factors.

Beyond price discretion, the importance of pricing skill depends upon the size of a firm's net profit on sales. If, for example, its profits are very low, then a tiny increase in price might result in a spectacular increase in net profits. Conversely, when net profits on sales are already large, a small increase in price will not produce a substantial increase in profits. The

EXHIBIT 2

Main Determinants of Price Discretion

Customer Concern with Price	Similarity of Sellers' Offerings		
	Identical	Modest Differences	Large Differences
Slight concern	No discretion	Considerable discretion	Great discretion
Moderate concern	No discretion	Modest discretion	Substantial discretion
Overwhelming concern	No discretion	Slight discretion	Slight discretion

matrix in Exhibit 3 combines price discretion and the rate of profits on sales to account for the contribution of pricing skill to business success. As our discussion has implied, its importance is greatest where price discretion is great and profits on sales are low. Where the firm possesses little or no price discretion, pricing skill has very little or no importance. The greater the current rate of profits on sales, the less its importance.

It may be said that a majority of firms occupy a position in which pricing skill will affect profitability very greatly. Why? Because sellers' offerings are dissimilar and many—but far from all—customers are quite concerned about price. Thus we see that the importance of price to a firm's success may be great—which need not mean, however, that it is difficult to set price.

Little has been written about the ingredients of pricing skill. Does a pricer require mastery of economic theory? Of demand forecasting techniques? Of game theory? Although this question is impossible to answer in a sentence, the main requirement for pricing excellence seems to be skill in the application of decision theory and marketing concepts.

PRICING SUCCESS AND THE FORMULATION OF PRICING OBJECTIVES

Many objectives may be achieved by creative pricing, and many of these are overlooked by most executives responsible for pricing. Pricers tend to recognize only a direct financial objective: to secure full payment for the benefits that their firm offers to their customers.

EXHIBIT 3

IMPORTANCE OF PRICING SKILL IN BUSINESS SUCCESS

Net Profit on Sales	Price Discretion			
	None	Slight	Substantial	Great
High	Very low	Low	Slight	Modest
Medium	Very low	Slight	Modest	Substantial
Low	Very low	Modest	Substantial	Great

It is possible to identify a fairly long list of pricing objectives—on a variety of levels. Most of these objectives are instrumental; that is, they contribute to long-range profits but do not produce higher profits directly. By identifying these instrumental goals for pricing, the price setter gains direction and guidance.

For example, pricers may endeavor to set prices that will induce customers to prefer their brand over others and to pay a premium for their brand. Can a firm influence the number of purchases and customer willingness to pay premiums by the price it charges? The answer would seem to be positive, for prices can be set in a way that conveys the message of high quality and thereby enhances a brand image. A further goal is to set prices in ways that make them appear "fair" and that make the firm seem fair in its dealings. This too would seem possible. There is even considerable evidence that some prices are psychologically attractive for reasons that are obscure.

One should, of course, arrange pricing objectives in the form of a hierarchy, for these—and related—goals are not on the same level. The following series may constitute one possible hierarchy:

1. Get the maximum total revenue over total cost that customers will pay.
2. Do so by creating an impression that your brand offers greater value than rival brands.
3. Convey the impression that your company's prices are about the same as those charged by other firms—when they actually are higher.

Customer Classification for Pricing Purposes

All customers do not respond similarly to a seller's actions. For example, one cannot assume that all potential buyers will be more likely to buy an item as a result of a reduction in its price. Some people may interpret the price decline as evidence of a reduction in quality or of the brand's being held in general disfavor.

Such differential—here contradictory—responses of customers to the same action by the seller are sometimes designated as the result of "incompatible customer segments." The central point to recognize is that customers cannot all be considered similar for pricing purposes. Consequently, those responsible for pricing ordinarily would be wise to classify their potential customers.

The following list suggests some potentially important distinctions among customers for pricing purposes. In recognizing and capitalizing on these differences, price setters are likely to adopt novel approaches and actions. Customers for most products differ in—

1. Sensitivity to price reductions—desire to "get a bargain."
2. Sensitivity to changes in absolute level of price.
3. Price "bracket" ordinarily patronized and strength of commitment to that price bracket.
4. Degree of price awareness—speed with which price changes are noted.
5. Need for reassurance about "goodness" of price—reflected in number of price comparisons before and after purchase.
6. Knowledge of prices charged by different sellers.
7. Strongest associations with price:
   a. Product characteristics associated with high, medium, and low price.
   b. Attributes of seller and product used as cues to relative level of price.
8. Present feelings about fairness of prices charged—for all brands in general.
9. Expectations of future price movements for product and brand.
10. Views about magnitude of price differences to be found in market for item in question at any given time.
11. Pleasure gained in buying at a low price and pain suffered at "overpaying."
12. Degree of mistrust of seller—fear of being overcharged.
13. Confidence in ability to judge quality and value.
14. Concern with periodic payments on credit purchases rather than with purchase price.

✦　✦　✦

It is perhaps paradoxical that so little is known about the role of price in our economy and about the management of price for private profit. After all, economists have been preoccupied with price almost to the exclusion of anything else.

Economic events, institutions, and viewpoints have changed greatly in recent decades. We cannot hope to understand and manage existing arrangements by a near-religious faith in traditional theory. A fresh and honest look at market processes is required—especially by those who have struggled to cope with them. At the moment, we may possess too little factual knowledge about markets to develop illuminating theories. But makers of public policy, price setters for business, and administrators of government regulations related to price cannot wait. At present they hold varied and conflicting views which rest on very fragile foundations.

Businessmen should be encouraged to be creative in their pricing. Even more, those who seek to understand and change the market process should feel obliged to explore—creatively—new theories and models.

Pricing Policy
and Objectives

Otto Wheeley

THE IMPACT OF PRICING ON A COMPANY'S SUCCESS AND FORTUNES CANNOT BE overstated. On the one hand, in a simple situation in which a product sells for one dollar with a 10-cent profit, a mere 10-percent increase in the price can double the profit. The leverage which such pricing has on the over-all profitability of the company is obvious. A company can also find itself caught in a downward spiral in which prices are cut throughout the industry about every three months in the mistaken notion that this will result in more business. One observer has described this kind of pricing as "disgraceful" management. Not only do such pricing decisions have an immediate effect on profits, but virtually all price changes have long-run influences that may be insidiously revealed only with the passage of time.

A MAJOR MANAGEMENT FUNCTION

A sound approach to pricing must begin with the understanding that the setting of price policies is a major management function. Traditionally,

OTTO WHEELEY is Vice President-Marketing for Koppers Company, Inc.

a great deal of thought and planning is given to engineering, manufacturing, advertising, and sales promotion activities. Certainly the same kind of careful study and planning must go into the formulation of price policies that best serve the long-term objectives of a business. In such a context, pricing based on well-formulated policies might truly be termed "creative" pricing, since major price decisions are not an expedient reflex to day-to-day crises in the marketplace.

In this age of rapid change, constant and continuing vigilance over policies and pricing strategies must be maintained. Pricing policies can become as quickly obsolescent as the products they represent. New products, new industries, new technologies demand equally creative pricing. Pricing policies, therefore, must be flexible enough to accommodate the changing competitive needs of the business yet consistently insure that the growth and profit objectives of the business are met.

A key point that must be emphasized once and for all is that not only must pricing be responsive to customer needs, but it must also take into consideration the needs of the company. No customer is best served if an important supplier goes bankrupt or is unable to meet unrealistic delivery dates. Thus sound pricing will often be a compromise reflecting the needs of many interested parties, external as well as internal.

DEFINING THE OBJECTIVES OF PRICING POLICY

There was a time when a businessman could say that his pricing was based on three simple objectives: (1) market his goods; (2) recover his costs; (3) generate a "reasonable" return on investment. That is still the starting framework. But this meager framework does not convey the complex relationship between prices and the many other elements of competitive strategy employed in modern business. Nor does it get to the heart of the pricing problem plaguing most industry today—that prices play an essential role in supporting long-term progress and growth.

The ultimate test of pricing policies is that they provide a reasonable return on investment over the long run. This rate will vary for a particular industry or a particular company depending on many factors, including its state of development, its growth potential, and the special economic climate in which it operates. For a company with a high capital investment a reasonable return should recover all costs, including the unofficial ones like the erosion of capital through inflation and the erosion of technology through rapid obsolescence. In addition, it should be sufficient to maintain the industry in vigorous health, able to anticipate changing demands and to build for growth. In short, as any good lumberman would say, "the cost of the tree is the forest regrown."

Determination of the appropriate rate of return may be exceedingly complex, however, and this in turn equally complicates the setting of price policies. A growth industry, for example, with its special risks and challenges, may require a considerably higher return on the funds committed to plant facilities and working capital than the average of all manufacturing. There also will be variations in the amount of return required for different areas of a company's investments, again depending on the stage of product development and process knowledge, as well as on the operating rate of the facilities. On a standard product, where practices are established and know-how is generally available, the margin required may not be much higher than the 10-percent return on investment earned as an average for all manufacturing companies. On new products, however, where there has been a large investment in development and unusual know-how, and a high capital and startup investment, a much higher return will be required to provide for regrowth and expansion.

There will also be a variation in the rate of return required depending on how completely a company's capacity to manufacture a product is being used. Appropriate pricing policy should permit a company to achieve reasonable rates of return at less than 100-percent operation. Not only is this imperative to take care of customers during periods of peak demand, but it is vital to the orderly growth of capacity for a product. When a company can achieve a reasonable rate of return only by operating at full capacity, it has lost substantial control of its flexibility.

IMPACT ON NATURE OF COMPETITION

Once it is accepted that the primary purpose of sound pricing is to provide a reasonable rate of return on investment, broader objectives can be identified. It must be clearly evident that pricing policies have a profound effect on the nature of the competition a company must face. Price policies must be established, therefore, with full recognition of their effect on both direct and indirect competition. If prices are held too high too long, the industry may attract companies which otherwise might not find it a natural area of activity. This can lead in turn to wide swings in capacity and prices in which the customer is alternately faced with a shortage or an oversupply of the product.

Failure to follow realistic pricing policies has led to radical changes in an industry. The phthalic anhydride business is a good example (phthalic anhydride is a major industrial chemical used in paint, plastics, and several other products). The problem was precipitated when a major company in a related but different field, attracted by the high going price for this chemical, announced its intention to enter the phthalic business at publicly predicted prices substantially below the going price. Immediately, this announced potential price cut was met by a second major producer, and a substantial price decline followed as one price cut after another was matched by companies in the industry. As a result, the price of this product dropped precipitously even before the new supplier had begun production. The industry was no longer able to sustain the high rate of return on investment previously experienced. Capacity actually declined relative to demand, which still continued to increase. Consumers were eventually faced with a shortage of supply which ultimately was solved only as productive capacity was increased in response to better price and profit potentials.

A more creative approach to pricing policy in this situation could have helped preserve the balance between supply and demand. The high profits in the short run attracted a variety of producers, but sooner or later price and productive capacity had to come back into balance. In the meantime, however, until equilibrium was restored, customers and producers alike paid a heavy toll in lost profits partly as a result of short supply.

In retrospect, it also was clearly evident that the maintenance of the high price of phthalic caused it to lose ground in some uses. One major market, alkyd resins for paints, responded only after the price had dropped and phthalic became more competitive in this product application. In similar fashion, a company may not be able to introduce a new product effectively because its price is too high.

PRESSURES ON PRICING POLICIES

Price-cutting actions and reactions such as occurred in the phthalic business are the antithesis of sound pricing policy. To cut prices when costs are moving upward, and to believe without real reason that total volume and profits can be increased as a result, can lead in the long run to a destruction of capital values and growth capability. Sound price policy recognizes that no company is an island and none can establish an exclusive domain in price cutting. Companies with heavy capital investments simply cannot permit a competitive price move to go unmatched with counteraction. The grave danger here is that such tactics are costly and may lead to a financial weakening of the whole industry as well as the company which originated the downward spiral.

When a company finds itself in a chaotic price situation, it must accept compromises on long-run price policies and at the same time look for alternative courses of action. In certain phases of the organic chemical industry, for example, a way had to be found to reach beyond destructive price competition. In the case of one product, there was great price instability as recently as a decade ago; there was, in fact, a price for every job. There was also the influence of the endless price competition of lower-quality products from another field whose prices could not be matched. The answer was to move into the development and promotion of a quality line, with which move has come the achievement of reasonable price stability and consistent price policy. It is significant that this field is now in an era of progress and growth and that a creative price policy has been a constructive factor in this development.

Resort to subterfuges or gimmicks will ultimately have the effect of breaking or destroying a company's otherwise sound pricing policy. Obvious ways by which sound pricing can be destroyed are such sometimes hidden price concessions as special freight allowances, unreasonably long credit terms, unrealistic quantity discounts, the pretense of selling off-grade or lower-quality material to rationalize a price discount, or under-the-table rebates. Often companies have to decide between the immediate promise of short-range tactics and the slower but fundamental gains of long-term consistency. This is the area in which a company is tempted to backslide from the solid bases that are part of a constructive marketing pattern—and slide off into definite, though masquerading, price cutting.

Any price policy, therefore, which makes a special exception to a company's normal published price policy is not a policy at all but an accident. Like most accidents, it can be costly, painful, and unproductive. This is the gray area of pricing in which the hurly-burly of competition often forces hasty decisions, pushes for adjustments, prompts temporary retreats, and invites other apparent deviations from stated policy. In short, it is the area in which creative pricing is born or destroyed, because it is here that management can detour, undermine, or compromise the principles of creative pricing which it has formally endorsed.

ALTERNATE POLICIES AND OBJECTIVES

Pricing policies and objectives must reflect the principle that prices are not the sole or even the primary competitive weapon used by a company. Management should have much more than price to sell. Its products should have design and application features, availability, quality refinements, use convenience, modern packaging, and other valuable advantages. These are real competitive values; most of them are as important as price in creating demand—perhaps even more so. A company must place the price of its product in proper perspective and systematically identify the competitive advantages which it has.

In the case of wood-treating chemicals several years ago, the industry was faced with a major decline in demand. The customers for these products were faced with radically shrinking markets, and this in turn adversely affected sales. The first step in evolving a sound pricing policy required recognition that price was not the most important factor influencing sales. The creative marketing strategy was to offer the customer a marketing service which helped to increase his market potential and his sales.

A comprehensive study of the end uses of the chemicals was made. Customers were then given detailed information on product features, the advantages of treated wood, and competitive obstacles. A plan of action, tailored to each of the industries served, was proposed to recover lost markets and to develop new ones. These customers in turn used the information with their own customers, and the result was a dramatic reversal of the downward sales trend.

A customer-oriented company must, as in this case, be able to look beyond its immediate customers to the markets which they serve in order to determine the prime selling points of a product. In so doing, it is much more likely to develop a creative and successful pricing approach.

It may also look to other key competitive factors such as superior technology or outstanding service. If a company can offer its customers lower costs resulting from new or superior technology, it is helping to make them more competitive and more profitable. A great many services can be offered which are designed primarily to reduce costs and increase profits for customers. For example, to complete a high dollar investment such as a basic oxygen furnace for a steel producer well ahead of schedule can mean substantially increased profits or greatly reduced costs to him because he is able to generate a cash flow and begin covering his overhead costs much earlier than planned. The company that can successfully perform in this fashion for any of its customers can expect to be rewarded with a premium for such service.

The specific services or benefits which a company can offer will naturally vary from industry to industry and from company to company within each industry. Each management must creatively identify the particular way in which it can serve its customers. Services can range from imaginative inventory policies and engineering assistance all the way to the location of a new plant. For example, the key service provided for one customer was the location of a raw-material plant as close as possible to his own. In this way he was assured of a steady source of supply with transportation costs virtually eliminated. Here, again, a company can have a great deal more to sell than price.

Pricing policy certainly has to reflect the importance of a number of factors; in fact, the interrelationships among these factors will have a major impact on pricing. In general, four might be cited: (1) technology—where does the company feel it stands technically in relation to its competitors? (2) marketing position—what are the company's strengths and advantages in the marketplace? (3) facilities—can the company compete favorably, given the existing state of its production facilities? and (4) raw materials—does the company have access to economical and steady sources of raw materials?

Each of the above considerations must be weighed carefully in the determination of pricing policy. A serious limitation in the case of any one factor may severely hamper the company's ability to compete at any price. For example, a company may be anxious and able to compete in a certain market, but it may lack direct access to basic raw materials. The company is thus placed at a considerable disadvantage as compared to competitors because its raw material costs are too high. It will be able to develop sound price policies and compete effectively only after it has resolved its raw-material problem. In like fashion, another company may be unable to compete effectively because it has serious limitations in the area of technology, marketing outlets, or production facilities.

New Products

An analysis of all the major elements of competition is required in pricing new products. Policies may vary quite widely from one product to another as each is introduced to the marketplace.

Every new product replaces something and competes with a variety of substitutes for the customers' dollars. Pricing strategy must thus be based on the needs of the marketplace and alternative ways of meeting these needs. If the new product meets a long-recognized need and can be mass-produced, pricing policy may be designed to penetrate the market quickly and extensively. If the product is a specialty item, or if the risks associated with it are high for any number of reasons, a slower, more cautious approach may be indicated. The pricing policy chosen to introduce a new product can, in fact, make it a technical success but an economic failure.

There are probably no pricing policies which are more complicated than those associated with new products. A certain rate of return may be established as an objective only to be tempered by competitive factors. Pricing strategy must provide for an appropriate recovery of development costs balanced against the technical and marketing sophistication of the company's competitors. It may reflect management's estimate of the willingness of customers to pay a premium for an anxiously awaited item. Unforeseen complications or even windfalls may result, once the product is on the market, and the company must be prepared to adjust its pricing to accommodate changed conditions.

Basis of Information

Pricing policies must be established on the basis of all the known facts. In a recent decision, existing price policy was questioned in the face of an increase by a competitor. The temptation to follow suit was strong.

Despite the desire for an immediate reaction, a correct decision obviously required a thorough review of the entire competitive situation. In the end, management's decision was *not* to follow suit and allow the price rise, because the review indicated that the increase was ill-timed and would ultimately prove to be wrong. The real decision for management centered around a factual question: Had indirect competitors improved their product to a point where they were now in a favorable technical position as compared to the companies in the traditional industry?

If this question could be answered affirmatively, then to increase price under the circumstances would be a serious mistake. Any decision to change existing price policy would have to reflect the true competitive situation accurately, and this could be achieved only by means of factual information. Indeed, the distinctive feature of creative pricing is that it is guided by purpose, planning, and method. It cannot be based on hunches, emotions, or misinformation.

The facts upon which sound pricing depends are often difficult to obtain and interpret. The accompanying table, showing the price ranges for two products in which plastics competed with other materials, points up some of the complications. There is an apparent inconsistency in the price spread between the polyethylene rope and the polyethylene garbage can. The prices for the respective plastic products may not give sufficient weight to the use value of the products in competition with other materials. Certainly the use value of a product must be consistently interpreted if the price policy is to be sound, but perhaps too often the assumption is made that the price of any finished article must compete in total dollars or cents with the material it seeks to replace.

The data in the table could also reflect the failure of pricing to give proper recognition to the respective cost-price relationships. The development of careful and accurate cost-price relationships is an important but complicated aspect of pricing policy. In this case the cost-price ratio accurately reflects the true values of the chemicals and plastics as representing substantial investments in creative research, in plant equipment, and in products with superior qualities. The determination of these costs, of course, is a far from easy task.

EVOLUTION OF PRICING POLICIES

Pricing policies may evolve as a particular strategy appears to be successful. As the first cautious explorations of a particular strategy gain acceptance and test-marketing of the approach produces a solid feedback, the strategy in effect becomes more firmly established as policy. This was certainly true in the marketing of the wood-treating chemicals mentioned earlier.

In this case it was determined that the proper approach was to become, in essence, the marketing arm of those customers who were not so well equipped to carry out an extensive marketing program. Sound pricing

Price Ranges: Plastics vs. Competing Materials

	Raw Material	Manufacturer's Sales Price	Added Value Raw to Manufacturer's Sales Price	Retail Price	Added to Value Raw to Retail Price
	(Per Foot)	(Per Foot)		(Per Foot)	
ROPE:					
Wire, 6-strand, ½" std.	$0.06	$0.189	215%	$0.225	275%
Low-pressure polyethylene, ½"	0.0235	0.089	278%	0.108	359%
	(Per Unit)	(Per Unit)		(Per Unit)	
GARBAGE CAN:					
Galvanized sheet, 20-gal.	0.819	3.83	367%	6.35	675%
High-pressure polyethylene, 20-gal.	2.38	5.80	143%	12.95	444%
Galvanized sheet, 10-gal.	0.504	2.88	471%	4.95	892%
High-pressure polyethylene, 10-gal.	1.16	2.69	131%	5.95	412%

Source: Price records, Koppers Company, Inc.

policy was a recognition that price was not the most important factor influencing the sale of the products. Particular conditions in this industry provided an excellent opportunity for a creative marketing policy. As it evolved, the customers accepted the assistance of the supplier; and, eventually, this marketing strategy developed into a major policy.

PRICING POLICIES AND COMPANY IMAGE

Finally, it must be recognized that pricing policies are an integral part of a company's image. They help shape that image and, in fact, may be a major factor in determining it. The field sales force at the same time must be trained to resist price decrease requests by selling the company's pricing policy and the product's advantages. Customers who are reassured that prices are being administered uniformly and fairly will accept the fact that their competitors are not getting a better price.

The customers' best interests may not really be served by wheel-and-deal price fluctuations, and they may be just as unhappy with uncertainty about price as are the producers. At a trade association convention, for example, a number of houseware molders gave vent to severe criticism of the price practices of the producers who were supplying them with plastic materials. One customer was quoted as follows:

> When you producers were selling polyethylene to us molders at the stable price of 41 cents a pound, my company made more money than we do now, when the price is much lower but bounces up and down with every deal. Why? Simply because I didn't have to spend all my time rushing around to see if I could make as good a deal as the next guy—and never being quite sure. Nowadays I'm too busy trying to be a price detective to get any constructive work done. Like any buyer, I want the lowest price reasonably possible, but if it has to be at the expense of my peace of mind and the creative side of my work, then I'll take the stable price even though it is higher.

Salesmen must be made to realize that they cannot rely on price maneuvering to win and retain customers. Over the longer run, a salesman who encourages price cutting will lead his company into competing with itself because customers will doubt its basic integrity. Salesmen should be taught to explain to customers the fairness of consistent price policy; thus they become more than messenger boys parroting prices and, in fact, have the opportunity to sell the solid features of the policies themselves. At the same time, they help to promote the integrity of the company. In the final analysis poor salesmen can erode price policies, which, in reality, are only as good as the salesmen who work with them.

✦   ✦   ✦

The benefits of creative pricing have a broad base, extending through individual companies and industries and affecting the health and vigor of the whole economy. A consistent price policy will give more assurance and stability to planning for the future. As the housewares molder pointed out, it allows staff to devote more time and energy to really creative activities. It clears the way for physical expansion, for new product development, for more efficient production, for more useful product applications, and for better earnings performance. A company that can sell both dependable products and dependable prices can help eliminate the "feast or famine" situation that often prevails in price-only competition.

Finally, holding firm to a consistent price policy can do more toward strengthening and stimulating this nation's economy than any government planning group can ever hope to achieve.

Pricing:
Whose Responsibility?

Donald B. Tuson

THE RESPONSIBILITY FOR ANY COMPANY'S PRICING POLICY MUST BE VESTED IN the chief executive officer. He may delegate the legwork needed for studying, proposing, and reviewing pricing policy, but he cannot delegate the job of deciding what it will be. Pricing has too much of an effect on his company's success.

The legal aspects of pricing are best left to the company's attorneys. The theoretical effects on the economy as a whole and on overall supply and demand are best debated by trained economists and college professors—and one may doubt whether pricing policy in one company does invariably affect the market in quite the way that these and other students of the scene would like to have us believe. In short, it is not so much the sociological impact of pricing as it is the direct influence on the company's profitability that must concern the chief executive. Only he can have the final say.

DONALD B. TUSON is Vice President-Finance, Carling Brewing Company, Cleveland, Ohio.

A Matter of Balance

Among the primary duties of the chief executive officer is that of seeing that his company's production, distribution, and financial capacities are not too far out of balance at any one time. If one or more of these three areas does create an imbalance of any duration, the chief executive knows that the company will be in trouble. And unrealistic pricing policies *can* bring about an imbalance in any or all of these areas.

In too many organizations, marketing success is judged on the basis of volume. The quickest way to improve volume temporarily may be through price cutting. Gross inefficiency apart, however, the one tool that one's competitors can meet is price cutting, and even an inefficient competitor can usually meet unrealistic prices for a long period of time by living on his cash flow. The chief executive officer must therefore take great pains not to be pressured by marketing and sales management into unrealistic and uneconomic pricing decisions.

Prices, it is safe to say, are commonly determined more by what someone else feels they should be than what company executives feel they should be. Although we like to think that managements are becoming more sophisticated about the economics of their businesses, there are still many that appear to have little knowledge of costs and profits except from a total corporate standpoint. They either cannot or do not consider it worthwhile to relate the out-of-pocket costs of producing, distributing, and financing to revenues derived from specific products, territories, or volume. Also, there are many companies that are compelled to sell their products at cost—or less than cost—merely to stay in business.

When these conditions exist, it becomes extremely difficult to price on the basis of cost and desired profit. The stronger companies must base their prices on their evaluation of how long underpriced competition can hang on and what prices can be charged without losing too much volume to the underpriced competitors. To make this evaluation realistic, they must have a knowledge of the low-priced competitors' production capacities, those competitors' approximate out-of-pocket costs, the extent to which such out-of-pocket costs limit the areas in which the low-priced competitors can sell, and how long the low-priced competitors can sell at little or no profit. In addition, making certain that pricing policies are legal is a continuing consideration.

Pricing at cost or below total cost may allow one company to gain a larger share of the market or to hold its present share of that market. In the long run, however, selling at cost or below cost cannot be effective without sacrificing product quality and damaging production, distribution, and financial capacity.

QUANDARY FOR THE CHIEF EXECUTIVE

It is not difficult to understand, then, that the chief executive who has the final say on pricing can be in a continuous quandary. He is pressured from one direction by marketing and sales personnel, who usually think mostly in terms of what competition is doing with respect to volume and market share. He is pressured from another direction by production personnel, who think in terms of production scheduling and costs. Finally, he must face his financial people, his board of directors, and his stockholders, who think in terms of what prices will do to earnings and return on investment.

Without some method of evaluating proposed price changes as they are likely to affect total corporate operations and profits, the chief executive officer cannot reach logical decisions. Therefore, even though he must have the final say, it is up to financial and planning personnel to present facts and estimates that will allow him to make sound decisions.

Consider, for example, the chief executive of a company that manufactures a popular packaged food item. It may be a favorite breakfast cereal, a soft drink, or a dessert powder. In determining pricing policy, this manufacturer has a problem quite different from that faced, say, by the supplier of the materials that become unidentifiable parts of the end product. Price will depend more on brand name, and on the image and price of substitute items, than on the costs of production. Packaging also will be a factor; costs here are often as high as production costs—or higher. In fact, manufacturers of consumer products like to say, ruefully, that they are in business as much to make money for the container and package manufacturers as for themselves.

Be that as it may, how much the consumer-product manufacturer can realize for his product is likely to be determined, in general, by

1. What the customer is used to paying for identical or similar products.
2. How much of the spread between costs and the price to the con-

sumer must be shared with retail stores, distributors, commission agents, and others in the chain of distribution. This usually depends on how much they require as an incentive to display and promote the product.

3. The extent to which packaging and container manufacturers can influence the consumer to demand convenience packaging and pay the increased costs that result from such packaging.

GOAL: A REALISTIC RETURN

Generally, for a manufacturer, there is no one price for a product. There is a mix of prices that he receives depending not only on size and type of container and/or package but on where he is selling and on local market conditions. Thus, in establishing pricing policy, the manufacturer must be in a position to evaluate the probable effects of each pricing decision in each market. He must be able to make reasonable judgments as to the effect on immediate and long-term volumes and profits.

Since production and distribution costs for our consumer-product manufacturer vary substantially by size and type of container and package, and since the consumer has her own criteria for what she will pay (based not only on the quantity and quality of cereal, beverage, or pudding she hopes to obtain but also on her ideas as to what constitutes proper packaging), the prices that can be charged do not necessarily vary in direct proportion to total production and distribution costs. Therefore, management's efforts might reasonably be directed toward some such goal as the following: to maintain a sufficient spread between selling prices and direct costs of total volume to recover all common costs and provide a predetermined return on total assets employed.

In working toward this realistic return on investment, extensive distribution cost analysis is essential both before and after the fact. Our manufacturer must realize that both his pricing and the spread between selling prices and direct costs will depend largely on local competition. He cannot for long price his product in any market higher than his competitors. He may, of course, be the one who is holding the price down, in which case he cannot price the product so low that his margins will not substantially cover the direct, out-of-pocket costs of making and selling that product. Hence the wisdom of a corporate policy that revenues must exceed direct production costs for each package in each market and that total revenues from packages sold in a particular market must exceed total direct production costs and out-of-pocket selling costs for all packages sold in the market.

To be sure, these requirements may be modified in a certain number of "opportunity" or "investment" markets where the company is trying to introduce its products. But, here again, management must from the beginning adopt a pricing policy that will not leave the consumer with the impression that he can get something for nothing. Not, that is, if the company wants its product accepted as a quality, competitively priced item.

THE USE OF A PRICING COMMITTEE

True, competition largely determines price. On the other hand, the management of any company likes to feel that it is quite as able as its competitors to operate within established price limits. In a high-volume low-profit business like packaged foods, a price decrease of a penny per case can mean the loss of substantial sums. Pricing, in short, is a serious matter.

For this reason, to assist the chief executive in making his pricing decisions, a company might very well consider the establishment of a pricing committee. In the multidivisional, geographically dispersed company, there might even be a national committee and several divisional committees, each of the latter reporting to its divisional vice president or other chief executive.

The divisional pricing committee, in addition to the division head, normally includes the division marketing director, the division controller, and the division planning director. They are responsible for

1. Continuously reviewing competitive pricing activity and keeping the national committee informed on it.
2. Continuously reviewing prices and profit-contribution objectives for each version of each of the company's products.
3. When, after comprehensive study, it seems to make sense, recommending price changes to the national committee. Such recommendations must be accompanied by supporting statements of logic and by estimates of how the recommended changes will affect volume and profits.
4. Recommending prices for new packages to the national committee.

When pricing recommendations are to be prepared, the bulk of the work is done jointly by the divisional planning manager and the divisional controller. The division chief must give his approval.

The national pricing committee reviews all divisional pricing recommendations. It either passes them along to the president for approval or disapproves them and returns them to the division. The members of the national committee might include the executive vice president, vice president-finance, vice president-legal, vice president-production, vice president-marketing, and vice president-planning. Administrative detail could be handled by a director of marketing administration and pricing or similar functionary, who also would act as secretary of the committee.

Although the reasoning behind this suggested pricing-committee membership is obvious, it should be pointed out that each man plays a more important part in some pricing decisions than he does in others. The vice president-legal must satisfy himself as to the legality and possible legal consequences of every pricing proposal. The vice president-finance looks at every recommendation to ascertain that a logical approach has been taken in estimating the short- and long-term effects on profit contribution. The vice presidents in charge of production and planning are especially interested in decisions that may result in volume changes or swings in mix.

As a whole, the national pricing committee must endeavor to take a broadly general management approach. What will be the effect of this decision, it must ask itself continually, on our production, distribution, and financial capacities and, above all, our total profits?

PRICING AND THE PROFIT PLAN

Finally, it is entirely possible that pricing decisions will be controlled by company profit plans.

Once each year, many organizations go through the exercise of developing volume and earnings objectives for markets, region, or division and for the overall company. This may involve quite complex computer programs giving effect to assumed prices and mixes, industry growth rates in specific markets, seasonal trends, and changes in market share. The result may be a final profit plan that in condensed form looks something like Exhibit 1.

As can readily be seen, Exhibit 1 is a pro forma income statement upside down. In it, "Desired Net Income" is based on the desired percentage of net worth or total assets employed, and "Estimated Federal Income Tax" and

EXHIBIT 1

A Profit Plan

	Consolidated		Territory X 10,000 Units		Other Territories 90,000 Units	
	Total	Per Unit	Total	Per Unit	Total	Per Unit
Desired Net Income	$ 100,000	$ 1.00	$ 10,000	$ 1.00	$ 90,000	$ 1.00
Estimated Federal Income Tax	100,000	1.00	10,000	1.00	90,000	1.00
Desired Net Income Before Provision for Federal Income Tax	$ 200,000	$ 2.00	$ 20,000	$ 2.00	$ 180,000	$ 2.00
Period Costs:						
Production	$ 400,000	$ 4.00	$ 50,000	$ 5.00	$ 350,000	
Administrative	200,000	2.00	20,000	2.00	180,000	
Financial	90,000	.90	10,000	1.00	80,000	
Total	$ 690,000	$ 6.90	$ 80,000	$ 8.00	$ 610,000	$ 6.77
Sales Must Exceed Variable Costs by	$ 890,000	$ 8.90	$100,000	$10.00	$ 790,000	$ 8.77
Costs That Vary with Volume:						
Production	$1,040,000	$10.40	$130,000	$13.00	$ 910,000	
Selling	160,000	1.60	18,000	1.80	142,000	
Administrative	50,000	.50	1,000	.10	49,000	
Financial	50,000	.50	1,000	.10	49,000	
Total	$1,300,000	$13.00	$150,000	$15.00	$1,150,000	$12.77
Sales Must Exceed Costs Incurred to Obtain Sales Volume	$2,190,000	$21.90	$250,000	$25.00	$1,940,000	$21.54
Costs to Be Incurred to Obtain Sales Volume	650,000	6.50	50,000	5.00	600,000	6.66
Required Sales	$2,840,000	$28.40	$300,000	$30.00	$2,540,000	$28.20

"Period Costs" are added to "Desired Net Income" to arrive at the figure shown as "Sales Must Exceed Variable Costs by"—which means, essentially, revenues reduced by variable or out-of-pocket costs. For example:

	Consolidated	
	Total	*Unit*
Required Sales	$2,840,000	$28.40
Less Variable Costs		
Costs That Vary with Volume	$1,300,000	$13.00
Costs Spent to Obtain Volume	650,000	6.50
Total	$1,950,000	$19.50
Sales Greater than Variable Costs	$ 890,000	$ 8.90

"Costs That Vary with Volume" refers primarily to those often classified as variable production costs. They can, however, include certain costs that might be considered to result from actually accepting orders.

"Costs to Be Incurred to Obtain Sales Volume" means advertising and promotion costs and salesmen's salaries, fringe benefits, travel and subsistence, and related costs. These are incurred for the purpose of inducing the customer to buy.

To arrive at "Sales Must Exceed Variable Costs by," many price/cost/volume computations are customarily made—by market, by region, by division, always assuming various prices, volumes, package mixes, and marketing-expenditure rates. Once a reasonable plan seems to have been reached, it is frozen. For example, Territory X in Exhibit 1 is expected to have its sales exceed variable costs by $100,000. This $100,000 is "sacred" regardless of what changes are made with respect to price, package mix, volume, and the like.

Exhibit 2 illustrates the type of presentation that might be expected from marketing and planning personnel under certain conditions. The primary purpose of requiring it is to emphasize to such personnel what happens as a result of changes in plans that they prepare.

As will immediately be apparent, the "Original Plan" column for Territory X ties into the profit plan for Territory X in Exhibit 1. The numbers are arranged differently because of the difference in emphasis. Notice, too, that in Exhibit 2 profit before tax is treated as a period cost. This is because, whatever changes are proposed in Territory X's marketing plan, the $20,000 profit before tax is sacred. It *must* be earned.

EXHIBIT 2

TERRITORY X

PROMOTION COSTS: ORIGINAL PLAN AND CHANGES

	Original Plan 10,000 Units		Change 1 — To Add 3,000 Units				12,572 Units to Break Even[e]	
			Plus 3,000 Units		Total for 13,000 Units			
	Total	Per Unit	Total	Per Unit	Total	Per Unit	Total	Per Unit
Sales	$300,000	$30.00	$(10,000)[a] $87,000[b]	$25.67	$377,000	$29.00	$364,580	$29.00
Less Costs That Vary with Volume:								
Production	$130,000	$13.00	$39,000[c]	$13.00	$169,000	$13.00	$163,436	$13.00
Selling	18,000	1.80	5,400[c]	1.80	23,400	1.80	22,630	1.80
Administrative	1,000	.10	300[c]	.10	1,300	.10	1,257	.10
Financial	1,000	.10	300[c]	.10	1,300	.10	1,257	.10
	$150,000	$15.00	$45,000	$15.00	$195,000	$15.00	$188,580	$15.00
Sales in Excess of Costs That Vary with Volume	$150,000	$15.00	$32,000	$10.67	$182,000	$14.00	$176,000	$14.00
Less Period Costs and Profit:								
Production	$ 50,000	$ 5.00	$ —	$ —	$ 50,000	$ 3.85	$ 50,000	
Administrative	20,000	2.00	—	—	20,000	1.54	20,000	
Financial	10,000	1.00	—	—	10,000	.77	10,000	
Profit Before Tax	20,000	2.00	6,000[d]	2.00	26,000	2.00	20,000	
	$100,000	$10.00	$ 6,000	$ 2.00	$106,000	$ 8.16	$100,000	$ 7.95
Available for Promoting Volume	$ 50,000	$ 5.00	$26,000	$ 8.67	$ 76,000	$ 5.84	$ 76,000	$ 6.05

Change 1:

a Effect of decreasing selling price from $30.00 to $29.00 per unit (10,000 units X $1.00).

b Effect on revenues of adding 3,000 units at $29.00 per unit (3,000 units X $29.00).

c Effect on costs that vary with volume of adding 3,000 units:

  Production   (3,000 units X $13.00).
  Selling   (3,000 units X $ 1.80).
  Administrative   (3,000 units X $ .10).
  Financial   (3,000 units X $ .10).

d To provide for a minimum profit before tax on the incremental volume of $2.00 per unit (3,000 units X $2.00 per unit),

e Assuming that $26,000 additional spent for promoting volume and price cut to $29.00:

  Available for promoting volume $ 76,000
  Add period costs and profits — original   100,000
  $176,000

Units required to contribute $176,000 of revenues greater than variable costs at $14.00 per unit ($176,000 ÷ $14.00 = 12,572).

Beyond these few observations, it is hardly necessary to discuss Exhibit 2 in any detail. With study, it should be self-explanatory. It illustrates a price-reduction proposal which, on the basis of marketing estimates, will add 3,000 units of volume, will add $45,000 to costs that vary with volume, can provide $6,000 of additional before-tax profit, and thus can give marketing $26,000 more to spend for promoting volume. It also demonstrates that if marketing spends $26,000 more to promote volume, it will take 12,572 of the 13,000 units projected after the change to break even—that is, hold the $20,000 before-tax profit called for in the profit plan.

The final, most emphatic figure in Exhibit 2 relates to costs "Available for Promoting Volume." It is synonymous with "Costs Incurred to Obtain Volume" in Exhibit 1.

The marketing plan for Territory X must obviously give full weight to pricing considerations. Moreover, since profit before tax and period costs are considered fixed, any price changes—as well as volume increases or decreases or changes in mix—must be analyzed for the probable effects on "Costs That Vary with Volume" and amounts "Available for Promoting Volume." Thus management controls price and its impact on operations and profit before the fact.

Any company must, as a minimum, earn what its major competitors are earning as a percentage of sales and as a return on total assets employed. If it cannot do as well as its competitors under its pricing policy and methods, it is doing something wrong.

Over any one- or two-year period, problems may arise that will not allow the company to do as well as its competitors. These problems must be regarded as only temporary, however. They must be solved quickly if the company wants to stay at all attractive to its stockholders and the investment community in general. And, each year, it must improve its efficiency —in pricing as in other management functions—and thereby hope to show still greater improvement in profit performance.

The Importance of Costs
in Pricing Decisions

Morton Backer

PRODUCT PRICING IS A COMPLICATED ART INVOLVING MANY CONSIDERATIONS: elasticity of demand, level of operations, inventories on hand, financial condition of the firm, inter- and intra-industry competition, product uniqueness, government restrictions, foreign imports, and so on. In this chapter, our primary concern is with the cost-price relationship. Yet it should be stressed at the outset that cost is only one factor in pricing.

There is a tendency to either underrate or overrate the importance of costs in pricing. The frequently repeated statements that "prices are based on competition" and "prices are based on costs" are equally inaccurate. Both costs and competition have important roles in pricing strategy. Their relative importance depends on the nature of the industry, the product, and existing market conditions. In many situations costs will have little direct impact on prices. In fact, prices may even establish costs rather than the reverse. This is clearly the case in joint-cost industries such as meat packing,

DR. BACKER is Professor of Accounting, School of Business Administration, University of Massachusetts, in Amherst.

petroleum, and certain mining operations, where costs are allocated to products on the basis of sales values. In these industries prices are influenced by world markets, interindustry competition, and long-term supply and demand. Cost also is less important in highly competitive industries, such as agriculture, where product differentiation does not exist, where the production cycle is extended over long periods of time, and where goods are subject to rapid deterioration.

When a new product is introduced into the line, management must decide whether it is more desirable to price the item for long-run cost recovery (inclusive of a reasonable profit) or to resort to a lower penetration price with little or no immediate profit. If the product has unusually attractive features or is patent-protected, management may even decide to reap a large profit at its inception. Costs should have a strong role in decisions to introduce a new product and in related decisions to continue or discontinue an item, in determining which products should be "pushed," and in the establishment of price differentials.

In general, the influence of costs on prices is most direct when a company's products are sufficiently different from those of competitors to permit pricing discretion. This applies not only to products with peculiarly identifiable characteristics but also to products for which such images have been created in the minds of customers through advertising. Costs also are important in monopolistic situations. Monopolies, of course, generally are subject to some form of rate regulation; and cost justification, as the basis for rate increases, must conform to prescribed rules or standards.

ECONOMIC PRICE THEORY

Economists have long been concerned with the nature and role of prices. In fact, price theory constitutes the mainstream of economic thought regardless of whether the business environment is relatively free or government-regulated. In a "free" enterprise society, price acts as a kind of omniscient regulator of the forces of supply and demand. In a socialist economy, prices are established by administrative decision and used as an instrument for allocating resources.

According to classical economic theory, under pure competition an equilibrium market price is achieved when the price at which the quantity of goods demanded by consumers equals the quantity offered by suppliers. If an excess of supply exists, prices will decline and marginal suppliers will be forced to withdraw. If more goods are demanded than are available, prices will rise and new firms will be attracted to the industry.

Despite the prominent role occupied by price theory in classical and neoclassical economic thought, pricing practices rarely conform to the traditional model. The postulates on which classical price theory is based are not compatible with the real world in which we live. They include such assumptions as perfect competition, substitutability of products, mobility of labor, fluidity of capital, knowledge of profitable opportunities, full-capacity level of operations, and the measurability of demand elasticity. In a society characterized by uncertainty and imperfect competition these postulates either are nonexistent or exist only to a limited extent. Contemporary economists of course are aware of these conceptual simplifications. Many even question the assumption of profit maximization in the short run. Nevertheless, the classical price model serves as a point of departure for predicting the effect of variations in a dynamic economy.

Each firm is confronted by a demand schedule for its products. The quantity demanded varies with the sacrifice—that is, price—which consumers are willing to endure in terms of other products or services forgone. This of course depends on their utility preferences. While economists have developed elaborate theories to explain the demand function, efforts to measure marginal utility have proved elusive. Yet two aspects of demand, elasticity and shifts, of necessity must enter into the thinking of the rational pricing executive.

The extent to which the number of product units demanded varies with a change in price is referred to as elasticity of demand. This is affected by innumerable factors including consumer needs, substitutability of other products, disposable income, postponability of purchases, advertising expenditures, and the like. Unfortunately, in practice, elasticity of demand rarely can be measured with precision. Nevertheless, whether through past experience with price changes, limited experimentation, or market research, the pricing executive cannot avoid an assessment of elasticity of demand.

The role of costs in pricing is not unrelated to the demand schedule. Where demand is relatively inelastic, cost increases can more readily be passed on to customers. In such situations, the effect of cost fluctuations on profit must be carefully analyzed. Price inelasticity does not necessarily mean that an individual firm can adjust prices with impunity. The reactions of competitors or of the government—that is, in the case of rate-regulated industries or commodities considered basic to the economy—still act as an important price constraint. Where product uniqueness exists, a company can more readily pass on cost increases to its customers. And, in industries where products are undifferentiated, this may be accomplished through judicious price leadership. Even in situations where the government's role is active, cost increases unrelated to operating efficiency represent a supportable basis for price justification. Where demand is elastic and the firm has some pricing discretion, that price should be sought which optimizes the cost-volume-profit relationship.

A shift in demand occurs when the character of a demand schedule is altered; in other words, at a given price a different quantity than previously is demanded. This may occur as a result of changing consumer preferences, fluctuations in income levels, new products introduced, tax and monetary policies, population trends, and so on. The firm may also induce shifts in demand by advertising, selling effort, and redesign of products. Since these efforts all involve expenditures, costs play a role in induced shifts in demand. In theory, at least, these cost outlays are justified only if the revenues resulting from the shift in demand exceed the costs incurred. In practice, this is most difficult to measure, and such decisions are based largely on intuitive judgment.

In order for a firm to remain in business, its long-run price must at least equal its cost of production inclusive of an adequate return on capital provided. Here, at least, the role of costs is abundantly clear. Yet all too often the business executive is compelled to rely on costs generated by the accounting system, which, as we shall see, may be inappropriate. Moreover, questions as to what constitutes a reasonable return on capital invested and how this is to be introduced into the price structure raise difficult conceptual and procedural problems.

In the short run, profits are maximized at that price at which the marginal revenue equals marginal cost; that is, the increase in cost of the last unit produced is equal to the revenue derived from its sale. This represents the firm's optimum level of operations. If marginal revenue exceeds marginal cost, additional income may be derived by producing and selling more units. However, cost accounting systems in practice generate average rather than marginal costs. It is important, therefore, for pricing executives to understand that in short-run pricing decisions an incremental- rather than average-cost approach is required.

To a considerable extent, pricing practices in this country conform to what Gardiner C. Means once referred to as "administered prices."[1] Instead of reacting to short-run market conditions, in conformance to classical economic theory, prices generally are established by administrative action and remain fixed for relatively long periods of time. In many of our basic industries—for example, copper, aluminum, rubber, steel, and oil—products tend to be similar and a few companies are dominant. In these oligopolistic situations, a price reduction by one company is quickly matched by competitors, and a price increase without corresponding action by competitors results in a sharp decline in unit sales. Thus there is no incentive for an individual company to deviate from the established price schedule. Price changes, when they occur, generally are a reaction to a cost-price squeeze or to interindustry or foreign competition which affects all companies in the industry.

The effect of cost increases on prices is reflected in such news items as the following:

> The Ford Motor Company raised its 1968 car prices Wednesday an average of $114, or 3.9 percent, over the prices on 1967 models.
>
> Earlier General Motors Corporation raised its average prices $110 or 3.6 percent; Chrysler Corporation, $133 or 4.6 percent; and Volkswagen, the German carmaker that is the fourth largest automobile seller in America, $48 or 2.6 percent.
>
> Despite the price increase, Ford said that the "prices of 1968 models reflect a partial offset only for cost increases incurred to date."
>
> The company said that it "has been faced with steadily rising labor and material costs."[2]

Cost Relevance

To the extent that costs are used in pricing, what kind of costs are needed? Accounting costs as such will not suffice; certain modifications are necessary. Costs must be purposive; they must be selected with a view toward solving the specific problem under consideration. In its study of pricing practices, the National Association of Accountants has noted that "the concepts of cost which are most appropriate for pricing purposes differ in

---

[1] Means, Gardiner C., "Industrial Prices and Their Relative Inflexibility," Senate *Document No. 13*, Washington, D.C., January 17, 1935, p. 1.

[2] Flint, Jerry M., "Ford Car Prices Up $114 for 1968," *The New York Times*, September 22, 1967.

many respects from the concepts of cost used for cost control and financial reporting purposes."[3] Jules Backman, in his study of pricing policies and practices for the National Industrial Conference Board, comments that "the cost theory of pricing is a nice, comfortable, easy-to-understand explanation—until a few key questions are asked: How are 'costs' determined? What is included in 'costs'? Are past, present, or future costs included? How is the breakeven point determined? What time period is covered? What is done if your competitor has a higher or lower price?"[4]

All decisions are concerned with the future. Costs for decision making must be prospective rather than retrospective. Prices should recover costs expected to be incurred during the pricing period. How can this be accomplished? One large company establishes prices by means of a top-level committee in which different functional executives participate. It is the responsibility of these officials to present data regarding the probability of cost changes in their respective areas—as, for example, raw materials, personnel, advertising. In such a setting, the role of the cost accountant is important. He must be prepared to trace the effect of these future cost expectations on the company's revenue-cost-price relationship.

One of the most glaring deficiencies in the use of costs for pricing is the inclusion of depreciation based on the acquisition cost of the assets in use. Apart from the merit or lack of merit of the financial accountant's adherence to original cost for income measurement, product prices provide the funds not only for income distributions and growth but also for the replacement of assets. Yet only a handful of companies presently give effect to replacement costs in the data submitted to pricing executives.

An uncritical use of plant overhead rates in product costs used for setting prices is dangerous. Admittedly, the use of overhead rates tends to assure full cost recovery in the long run. However, overhead rates generally do not segregate fixed and variable costs, and this distinction is important in short-run pricing decisions. Moreover, plant overhead rates emerge out of a process of cost allocation which is highly judgmental. Plant overhead rates may be determined on the basis of actual level of operations, physical capacity, or a long-run normal level—with varying results. Overhead rates also generally exclude cost variances and certain excess costs. Since excess costs reflect plant inefficiencies, they normally should be excluded from the

[3] NA(C)A *Bulletin*, August 1953, p. 1673.

[4] Backman, Jules, *Pricing: Policies and Practices*, National Industrial Conference Board, New York, 1961, p. 35.

pricing model. However, certain variances—for instance, above-standard supply prices or unfavorable changes in pay rates for indirect labor—do have pricing relevance.

The accountant does not give formal consideration to imputed interest (interest not actually incurred) in his calculation of product costs. Yet there is nothing theoretical about imputed interest in certain pricing situations. In heavily mechanized and highly diversified companies, where the intensity of capital required to produce different products varies markedly, failure to include provision for interest on capital employed may produce a serious imbalance in the price structure.

Many costs incurred in the production, selling, and distribution of products are indirect and must be allocated to such products on a more or less arbitrary basis. Apart from pure joint-cost situations, where no logical basis for cost assignment exists, sizable lumps of cost such as factory overhead, research and development, and central administrative and selling expenditures are only indirectly associated with specific products. For example, in the drug industry it is exceedingly difficult to attach research expenditures to discrete products. Much of this effort applies to an entire line of products; other research is of a general rather than a specific nature; and, perhaps most important, not all research is successful. Consequently, efforts to allocate research to products entail substantial judgment.

Despite these limitations, it is difficult to visualize how pricing can be intelligent in the absence of product-cost information. The knowledgeable pricing executive uses costs as a guide in pricing decisions rather than as a rigid formula. He then modifies his cost-price-profit target by a subjective assessment of market conditions.

COST-PRICING METHODS

Although many rule-of-thumb procedures are used by pricing executives, this discussion will be concerned only with four of the more refined cost-pricing methods. They are (1) full-cost pricing, (2) marginal-cost pricing, (3) return-on-investment pricing, and (4) flexible cost pricing.

Full-cost pricing. Under full costing, selling prices are computed by adding to the total factory cost an allowance to cover selling and administrative expenses and profit. An illustration of the use of the full-cost method for an optical company appears in Exhibit 1. This company's objective is to recover total costs plus a 6 percent profit on such costs. Factory overhead is

EXHIBIT 1

FULL-COST METHOD OF PRICING
(RETURN ON SALES)

	FRAME X Amount	FRAME X % to Sales	FRAME Y Amount	FRAME Y % to Sales
Direct materials (quantities x net purchase price)	$ .360	29.0	$1.200	35.6
Direct labor (hours required x average hourly rate)				

Operation	Avg. Rate per Hour	Hrs. per Frame	Labor Cost per Frame
1A Blanking	$1.60	.0083	$.0133
1B Cut out eye	1.50	.0111	.0166
1C Cut off top	1.50	.0100	.0150
1D Cut off bottom	1.50	.0100	.0150
1E Cut out pad	1.45	.0090	.0132

	FRAME X Amount	FRAME X % to Sales	FRAME Y Amount	FRAME Y % to Sales
	$ .200	16.1	.500	14.8

Factory overhead (departmental overhead rates x direct labor hours per frame)

Department	Overhead Rate per Hour	Dir. Labor Hours per Frame	Overhead Cost per Frame
1. Blanking and cutting	$2.25	.0484	$.1089
2. Grooving and beveling	2.10	.0425	.0820
3. Stamping and bending	2.60	.0250	.0650

	FRAME X Amount	FRAME X % to Sales	FRAME Y Amount	FRAME Y % to Sales
	.340	27.5	.750	22.2
Cost to make	$ .900	72.6	$2.450	72.6
Selling and administrative expense (30%)	.270	21.8	.735	21.8
Cost to make and sell	$1.170	94.4	$3.185	94.4
Profit (6%)	.070	5.6	.191	5.6
Price	$1.240	100.0	$3.376	100.0

presumed to vary with direct labor hours. Selling and administrative expenses are assigned to products at 30 percent of factory costs on the basis of the overall ratio between these two cost categories.

The full-cost method is widely used as a basis for price setting; World War II created an impetus toward it. During the war we had not only governmental cost-plus-fixed-fee contracts but also price control, which sanctioned price increases according to prescribed cost formulas. Throughout hostilities and during the immediate postwar period, an unprecedented demand existed for consumer products. This permitted management to give prime consideration to cost recovery in pricing its products.

The obvious advantage of the full-cost method is that it assures total cost recovery. This is particularly important in long-run pricing. Despite its great popularity, however, there are definite limitations to full costing as a basis for pricing.

First, it ignores the elasticity of demand. While this rarely can be measured with precision, there are many occasions when a pricing executive can and must predict the effect of a change in price on the quantity sold. Since the full-cost method does not segregate the fixed and variable costs, it is not possible to see what effect a price change will have on profits.

Second, the full-cost method fails to give consideration to competition. A business does not operate in a vacuum. Management should not automatically assume that it performs as efficiently as its competitors and therefore can treat their lower prices with disdain. Instead, a firm should constantly strive to reduce its costs so that they will be equal to or lower than those of their rivals. Pricing at full cost tends to perpetuate existing inefficiencies by incorporating them into the price structure.

Third, the full-cost method does not distinguish between "out of pocket" and "sunk" costs. Thus a firm using this method may be inclined to reject orders which do not at the very least cover the total costs involved. However, as we shall see, the acceptance of such orders under certain conditions will increase rather than decrease profits.

Fourth, the full-cost method applies a flat percentage to the total cost of each product to allow for profit. Executives who use this method invariably state that the profit margin represents a "fair" return, but they have difficulty in defining what a fair return is without having recourse to other criteria such as invested capital. The full-cost method also fails to recognize that all products may not be able to earn the same profit margin.

Fifth, under the full-cost method no consideration is given to the capital investment required to produce, finance, and distribute individual products or product lines. Yet the real measure of business efficiency is whether a satisfactory return on invested capital is being earned. Recognizing the return on invested capital is particularly important in multiproduct plants where varying capital investments are required for the different products or product lines. Failure to give effect to interest on product-line capital under such circumstances may produce an unbalanced price structure and result in an insufficient recovery of funds to provide for dividends and growth.

Marginal-cost pricing. Marginal costs are added costs; costs which would not be incurred if a product were not made. They include raw materials, direct labor, variable factory overhead, and variable selling and administrative expenses. Marginal costing is particularly useful in profit planning and in short-run pricing decisions. Since, under full costing, there is no segregation of fixed and variable costs, we cannot tell what the profit will be for different products or product lines with changes in prices and

EXHIBIT 2

MARGINAL-COST METHOD OF PRICING

	Frame X	Frame Y	
Marginal costs			
Raw materials	$ .360	$1.200	
Direct labor	.200	.500	
Variable factory overhead	.120	.280	
Variable selling and administrative	.140	.360	
Total marginal costs	$ .820	$2.340	Out-of-pocket recovery price
Fixed costs directly applicable to products or product lines	.060	.205	
Direct product cost	$ .880	$2.545	Direct product recovery price
Allocated fixed costs	.290	.640	
Total product cost	$1.170	$3.185	
Profit (6%)	.070	.191	
Full cost price	$1.240	$3.376	Long-run price to provide for dividends and growth

NOTE: Fixed-cost rates were established at budget level. Fixed costs per unit will rise below budget level and decrease above budget level.

quantities sold. Under marginal costing, the effect of such changes can easily be traced. Management is thus provided with a more useful tool for profit planning and budgetary control.

Exhibit 2 shows how the same costs for Frames X and Y would appear under marginal costing. The out-of-pocket recovery price is the minimum price below which a cash loss is sustained. The direct product recovery price may be regarded as the long-run minimum price needed to recoup the cash costs together with those fixed costs directly related to product manufacture and distribution. It may be thought of as the price at which the product pays for itself. The full-cost recovery price represents the target long-term price which permits the product to recover its direct costs as well as its proportionate share of the company's overall fixed costs and the desired profit.

Exhibit 3 is an example of how a large food manufacturing company uses marginal-cost pricing. A special section of the controller's department prepares product-cost statements based on forecasts for the forthcoming quarter. These are then compared with the actual cost for the preceding quarter and, if a significant difference is noted, forwarded to the pricing executive for possible action. It will be noted that the actual price increase did not correspond to the rise in variable costs since market conditions as well as cost changes are considered.

From a pricing standpoint, the essential difference between marginal costing and full costing lies in the concept of cost recovery. Under full costing, prices are expected to cover total costs, inclusive of fixed charges. Under marginal costing, any contribution toward the recovery of fixed costs is regarded as better than none at all. Pricing under marginal costing is more flexible than full-cost pricing; a pricing executive has more latitude. His objective is to discover the price and volume which will maximize profits, provided the price is at least greater than the marginal, or out-of-pocket, costs. Orders that might be rejected because they don't cover total costs or yield an adequate profit might be acceptable under marginal costing. (See Exhibit 4.)

The distinction between fixed and variable costs which is made under marginal costing facilitates the preparation of breakeven analyses and thus provides the pricing executive with another useful tool. In Exhibit 5 we assume that fixed costs directly chargeable to Frame X amount to $11,600 and that allocated fixed costs amount to $56,200. The "point at which the product pays for itself" is that sales volume which exactly covers the vari-

EXHIBIT 3

A LARGE FOOD COMPANY'S USE OF MARGINAL COSTS FOR PRICING
(PRODUCT Z)

	Last Quarter (Actual)		Next Quarter (Budget)		Comments
	Per Cwt.	% to Sales	Per Cwt.	% to Sales	
Raw materials					Prices of materials expected to increase as indicated.
Packaging	$ 7.60	29.12	$ 7.74	28.89	
Manufacturing labor	2.51	9.62	2.51	9.36	
					Wage rates expected to increase 5%.
Holidays, sick leave, vacations, etc.	2.33	8.93	2.45	9.14	
Factory repairs and maintenance	.56	2.14	.59	2.20	
Other variable factory overhead (per cwt. net)	1.20*	4.59	1.20	4.48	
Variable delivery and warehousing (per cwt. gross)	.25	.96	.25	.93	
Variable commissions and discounts (per sales $)	1.60	6.13	1.60	5.97	
	2.61	10.00	2.68	10.00	
Total variable costs	$18.66	71.49	$19.02	70.97	
Selling price	26.10	100.00	26.80	100.00	Price increased $.70 per cwt.
Contribution to fixed overhead and profit	$ 7.44	28.51	$ 7.78	29.03	
Fixed costs:					Increase in fixed costs results from an expected decline in volume during next quarter.
Factory (per cwt. net)	$ 1.26		$ 1.29		
Delivery and warehousing (per cwt. gross)	1.46		1.48		
Other selling (per sales $)	1.84		1.89		
Advertising (per sales $)	.40		.46		
Total fixed costs	4.96	19.00	5.12	19.10	
Net profit	$ 2.48	9.51	$ 2.66	9.93	

* Based on most recent 12-month period.

able costs and fixed costs directly chargeable to the product. As sales increase beyond this point, the product contributes to the absorption of indirect fixed costs but does not earn profit until the breakeven point is crossed. This type of analysis is particularly useful to pricing executives in attempting to evaluate the effect of contemplated price revisions. Suppose that, at the present price of $1.24, sales of Frame X amount to $240,000 (193,550 units) and profit to $13,500. If the price is reduced by 10 percent,

EXHIBIT 4

APPLICATION OF MARGINAL-COST PRICING

Assume: A cash offer is received from a South American distributor for 30,000 Frames X at $.85 each, or $.39 below the domestic price. Additional shipping costs are estimated to amount to $.05 per frame. The company presently is operating at 75% of normal capacity.

Calculation of Order Profitability

A. Under full-cost method

Price	$ .850
Factory cost (Exhibit 1)	$ .900
Add: Shipping charges	.050
Total cost	$ .950
Loss per unit	$ .100
Number of units	30,000
Total loss	$ 3,000

B. Under marginal costing

Price	$ .850
Marginal costs	
Raw materials	$ .360
Direct labor	.200
Variable factory overhead	.120
Shipping charges	.050
Total marginal costs	$ .730
Marginal profit per unit	$ .120
Number of units	30,000
Increase in company profits	$ 3,600

EXHIBIT 5

Breakeven Analysis
(Frame X)

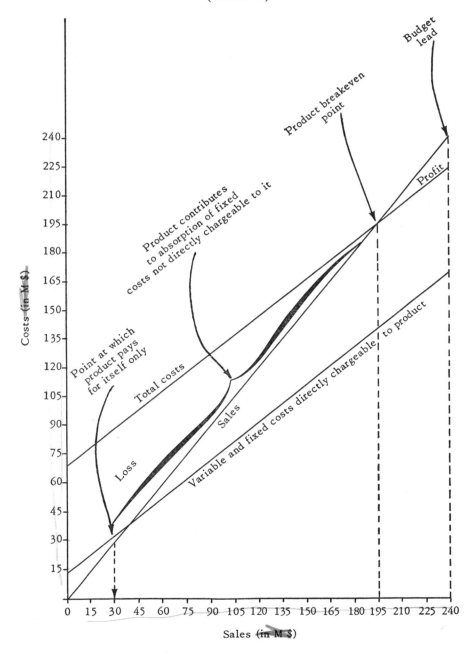

how many additional units must be sold to earn the same profit? This may be readily calculated.

Contemplated price $1.116
Contemplated contribution margin per unit $.296 (1.116 — .82)
Let x = number of units that must be sold to earn profit of $13,500

$$x = \frac{\text{Total fixed costs} + \text{desired profit}}{\text{Contribution margin per unit}}$$

$$x = \frac{67,800 + 13,500}{.296}$$

x = 274,660 units, or 81,110 additional units

Although this type of analysis is very useful in pricing decisions, care must be exercised. The cost-volume-profit relationship and the degree of variability of costs are not constant over time and should be frequently reviewed for changing trends.

Return-on-investment pricing. Most business firms measure the profitability of their products or product lines in terms of the return on sales. This is satisfactory for concerns in which the amount and turnover of capital invested in the various products are approximately equal. However, where different magnitudes of investment in working capital and facilities are required, the use of return on sales can lead to erroneous conclusions as to the real profitability of the product lines. In the final analysis, return on investment is the ultimate gauge of business efficiency.

Let us assume that the operating results for two products, *A* and *B*, are as shown below:

	A	*B*
Sales	$530,400	$982,800
Costs	408,000	756,000
Profit	$122,400	$226,800
Return on sales	23.1%	23.1%

Since both products show an identical return on sales, it would seem that they are equally profitable. However, if the average annual capital employed in production, selling, and distribution was $900,000 for Product A and $1,050,000 for Product B, the respective returns on capital would be 13.6 and 21.6 percent. Clearly, in terms of capital used, Product B is the more profitable item. Return on capital is equal to return on sales multiplied by the turnover of capital (sales divided by capital employed). Since return on sales is the same for both products, the difference in return on capital can only be due to capital turnover.

	Return on Sales	$\times$	*Capital Turnover*	$=$	*Return on Investment*
Product A	23.1%	$\times$	.589	$=$	13.6%
Product B	23.1%	$\times$	.936	$=$	21.6%

In this illustration, total return on total capital employed has been calculated for Products A and B. This involves allocations of both indirect costs and indirect capital. Such allocations can be avoided and a more precise measurement obtained by calculating *direct* return on *direct* capital used. Referring back to Frames X and Y, Exhibit 6 indicates how this might be

EXHIBIT 6

RETURN-ON-INVESTMENT METHOD OF PRICING

	Frame X	*Frame Y*
Direct capital required (at budget level)		
Receivables	$ 25,000	$ 15,000
Inventories	39,000	26,000
Facilities	14,000	15,000
Total direct capital	$ 78,000	$ 56,000
Direct product profit (at budget level)		
Sales	$240,000	$160,000
Less: Variable costs		
Raw materials	69,600	57,000
Direct labor	38,700	23,700
Variable factory overhead	23,200	13,300
Variable selling and administrative	27,100	17,100
Total variable costs	$158,600	$111,100
Marginal contribution	$ 81,400	$ 48,900
Less: Fixed costs directly chargeable		
to products or product lines	11,600	9,700
Direct product profit	$ 69,800	$ 39,200
Return of direct product profit on direct		
capital investment	89.5%	70.0%
Turnover of direct capital investment	3.1	2.9
% direct product profit on sales	29.1%	24.5%

accomplished. What constitutes an acceptable direct product return on direct capital used can be determined by equating this with the company's total-return-on-total-capital-employed target.

It should be noted that, like costs, capital employed varies at different operating levels. Certain capital, like fixed assets, remains relatively constant regardless of the level of activity. Other capital, like accounts receivable, varies directly with sales. A third category of capital, like cash and inventories, is partly fixed and partly variable. For example, a minimum cash balance is required to maintain even an inactive plant; but, as output rises, the cash requirements increase.

Flexible cost pricing. We have examined the three cost methods most commonly used in pricing decisions. These methods are not mutually exclusive. In fact, each of these cost-pricing techniques has certain limitations. The most effective system is one which can combine the salient features of these different methods. This would provide pricing executives with flexible cost data that can be used as a guide to pricing. As different competitive and internal conditions occur, they can select those costs and other quantitative criteria most relevant to the situation.

An example of this flexible approach, as used by a large container corporation, appears in Exhibit 7. The marginal ratio is particularly useful in short-term decisions when excess plant capacity exists and special price concessions to marginal customers will not disturb normal channels of distribution. The contribution ratio also may suggest a general price revision in a product line or specific product. Thus, in Exhibit 7, the decline in the contribution ratio is caused by an increase in variable costs. If this cost rise is industrywide, and if interindustry competition or other factors are favorable, the increase may be partially or totally passed on to customers. The direct profit ratio and pretax return on sales provide a means of measuring the adequacy of the price in terms of total cost recovery and profit earned. Direct and total return on capital employed provides an indication of the relative profitability of products in terms of the capital resources employed. This is useful not only in price reviews but also in capital-investment decisions; that is, those having to do with the expansion or contraction of facilities used to manufacture and distribute products. Capital turnover shows the extent to which capital assets are utilized. A low turnover ratio implies high capital intensity or unused capacity and may suggest a change in pricing strategy. Apart from its use in pricing, a report of this type contains valuable information for other important management decisions—for example, profit planning, performance evaluation, make or buy, and capital investments or disinvestments.

PRICE DIFFERENTIALS

The granting of discounts or other concessions to customers is an important aspect of pricing. Rare is the firm that does not indulge in at least some form of price differentiation. Price differentials are based on the assumption that customers can be segregated into classes and that the cost of serving each class varies. Differentials may be incorporated into the price structure of a firm through discounts or penalties based upon size of order, method of delivery, timing of sales, speed of collection, or distance from point of shipment. In addition to direct price concessions, differentials may

EXHIBIT 7

USE OF FLEXIBLE COSTS
BY A CONTAINER CORPORATION
(PRODUCT X)

	This Quarter		Last Quarter	
	Total	*Per Unit*	*Total*	*Per Unit*
Net sales	$680,000	$3.40	$748,000	$3.40
Variable costs	333,200	1.67	253,000	1.60
Contribution margin	346,800	1.73	396,000	1.80
Direct fixed costs	60,000	.30	58,000	.26
Direct profit	286,800	1.43	338,000	1.54
Allocated fixed costs	110,000	.55	112,000	.51
Net profit before taxes	176,800	.88	336,000	1.03
Direct product capital	380,000		395,000	
Allocated product capital	320,000		322,000	
Total capital employed	700,000		717,000	
Marginal ratio	51.0%		53.0%	
Direct profit ratio	42.2%		45.2%	
Pretax return on sales	26.0%		30.2%	
Direct return on direct capital	75.5%		85.6%	
Total return on total capital	25.1%		31.5%	
Direct capital turnover	1.79		1.89	

assume the form of cooperative advertising allowances, installation and repair services, return and trade-in policies, rebates, and so forth.

Price differentials often are based on industry practices; if so, the firm has no discretion regarding their establishment. When, however, a company is in a position to establish price differentials independently, cost analysis is most useful. In fact, the Robinson-Patman Act requires that volume discounts, for like items shipped interstate, be supported by provable cost savings. If price differentials are based on cost data, it is necessary, by measuring classes of revenue (for example, by size of order), to segregate those costs that are relevant and eliminable.

A Note on Mathematics

While it is beyond the scope of this chapter to examine the applicability of mathematical techniques of pricing, executives should at least be aware of their existence. Among companies that manufacture large and costly items such as air frames, turbines, and boilers, prices generally are established on the basis of negotiation. This is because each item or batch of items is made according to customer specifications and unit costs vary with the quantity produced.

In order to provide customers with price quotations, it is necessary to estimate costs in advance of production. This may be done by preparing a detailed bill of materials, estimating labor costs by operation, and applying a factory-overhead rate or rates. Past experience with similar items provides an important point of reference. Unfortunately, this procedure is not always satisfactory. First, the time and cost of estimating may be excessive, particularly when a large percentage of the quotations may not develop into firm orders and the cost-estimating effort may prove fruitless. Second, unit costs tend to decline, as the size of an order increases, because workers develop greater skill as they repeat operations and because startup costs can be amortized over larger quantities of product. Cost estimators long have sought a technique that would speed up the estimating procedure and also give effect to the size of the order on unit costs.

During the past 25 years, a new and valuable tool called the "learning curve" has been developed. This originated in the airframe industry but has since spread to other industries that produce costly equipment in which assembly labor represents a major element of cost. The learning curve is based on the principle that, as the quantity produced doubles, the cumulative average unit cost declines at a constant rate. The percentage of decline varies from industry to industry; but, in general, the higher the ratio of assembly labor to total cost, the greater the decline in unit costs will be with increases in quantity. The airframe industry has experienced an 80 percent learning curve. This means that, as production of an item doubles, the cumulative average production hours per unit for successive batches will be 80 percent of the preceding batch. With the use of logarithm tables and the computer, many advanced applications of the learning curve have been developed.

Effective pricing decisions depend upon marginal analysis, at least in the short run. However, calculating the marginal revenue function involves a host of interacting variables, including elasticity of demand, reactions of competitors to price changes, economic conditions, availability of substitutes, consumer knowledge, and extent of promotional effort. In recent years, some mathematicians and economists have attempted to deal with these uncertainties by the use of statistical sampling and the construction of probability models. An essential ingredient of these models is dependence on managers' subjective valuation of future probabilities. The combination of objective data and managers' subjective valuation can be expressed mathematically and an optimum profit path selected.

In some companies, literally thousands of items are ordered that have slight or substantial variations in conformance with customer requirements. In such situations, the cost and time of calculating cost estimates can be averted by setting up a matrix to reflect the different cost-pricing possibilities or by developing a mathematical formula which gives recognition to the variables involved.

Nonfinancial
Aspects of Pricing

Gordon T. Roberts

ANY ATTEMPT TO CONFINE PRICING TO THE FIELD OF ECONOMICS MUST, OF necessity, fail. Pricing transcends economics. It is infused with non-financial factors which have their bases in marketing theory, in social ethics, and in the theological concepts widely accepted within our culture.

Geographically, too, any endeavor to propound a worldwide pricing theory is bound to fail. It will be frustrated by the need to enunciate ancillary theories and exceptions which the marketer will experience internationally.

This chapter is therefore confined to a discussion which comprehends only larger businesses in the United States today selling consumer and industrial goods domestically. And, even with these restrictions, we are still confronted with such a great number of pricing situations as to defy ordinary generalization.

GORDON T. ROBERTS is an attorney, specializing in marketing law, with offices in Boston.

No Single System

Pricing arises out of the process of contract. Crudely defined, a contract is an agreement between parties to exchange considerations. Price describes the economic value, in terms of the accepted monetary means of exchange, of the buyer's payment in fulfillment of the sales contract. While it deserves attention in this context, the function of price *prior* to the formulation of the contract is also a main concern of the marketer.

The immensity of the problem of devising a general pricing theory, even one confined to the United States today, is apparent from the profuse literature in which theorists have capably discussed economic and "marketing for profit" pricing theory without proportional concern for pricing's social, psychological, and even theological aspects. Not only is there no one simple pricing system which can be expounded in an orderly fashion; but also, even were such an exposition available, no experienced marketer would need to be reminded that an orderly theory in this area would of necessity be disorderly in its real-life application.

Since no single "marketing for profit" economic pricing theory will satisfy the several pricing models inevitable for a business of more than modest size and complexity, we encounter alternative theories which often have different and sometimes rival features. For example, some fairly arbitrary cost-plus formulas may serve to handle the extensive replacement-parts offering of an industrial marketer, while a consumer marketer may need to focus on remaining competitive at the wholesale level of distribution in a manner consistent with an intelligent brand policy involving image, claim preemption, and retail end-digit psychology. Meanwhile, the construction industry can wrestle in competitive bidding to apply profitably the insights of classical game theory.

In this state of affairs, the practical marketer has little recourse but to define closely the competitive model within which he must price and to select from among the pricing theories available those ingredients which will permit the formulation of his own pricing policy and procedures. Needless to say, he will seek that policy and those procedures which, judgmentally, will bring his operation closest to the fulfillment of its operating objectives. This process may boil down to simply selecting a price which is "competitive." In this general context, then, pricing becomes a key element of the corporate plan which has final consequences which are measured principally in dollars and cents.

UNDERATTENTION TO NONFINANCIAL FACTORS

It is this highly ramified and variegated pricing theory, coupled with a tremendous urgency to achieve the financial results anticipated in the corporate plan (we note without serious prejudice that "the corporate plan" currently is becoming a sacred bull subject to quasi-religious management commitment, complete with an emerging planning priesthood) that results in the underattention accorded the nonfinancial aspects of pricing.

True, an examination of some of these aspects has its own peculiar problems. The intellectual satisfaction of observations concerning them is wanting because they do not fit into a Euclidian pattern as does, for example, marginal-price theory. Moreover, an acknowledgment of the existence of a particular nonfinancial pricing phenomenon may be interesting but of questionable utility. Busy marketers must always ask of the theory: "How can I use it? What do I do next?"

The buyer. It is, however, imperative that marketers pay due attention to those other elements of contractual consideration, apart from price itself, involved in the carrying out of the agreement to buy and sell. These are the nonfinancial factors of which we speak.

To illustrate, consider the seller of the permanent hair dye used widely today by fashion-conscious women. One of his distribution channels directs itself to supplying his product to the professional beautician who applies the coloring to her patron's hair. In pricing for sale to this market segment, the seller must take into account an important nonfinancial factor. The professional beautician, in selecting the seller's product for use, confers upon him more consideration than is represented by the monetary price paid; in addition, she effectively adds her professional appraisal of the quality and other features of his product. Therefore, when the seller considers this market segment in pricing, he must not only take into account competitive factors in that segment itself but also make a judgment as to the possible effect of the beautician's testimonial on the higher-volume retail market. Will increased sales of the hair dye through drug and cosmetic outlets, direct to women for self-application at home, result from the seller's having acquired a substantial share of the beauty-shop trade?

Some years ago, as a further example, a manufacturer was faced with a static share of the market for popular-priced pens. Through field research it was determined that a principal problem was the poor quality image of his brand. The seller recognized that his image might be improved—that is, the public might endorse his popular-priced pen—if he were successful in marketing a high-quality writing instrument as well. To this end, he designed and offered for sale a pen which he list-priced at more than ten dollars. The price of this new product was purposely set to yield a margin close to breakeven. This slim profit was a relatively low price, all things considered, for the buyer's enhanced view of the brand. The strategy resulted in a substantially increased market share for the high-volume, low-price product.

Other instances of the buyer's giving nonfinancial consideration to the seller are easy to cite. Among them we might mention the buyer who permits the seller to maintain a full product line, thus making it possible for the seller to attract competent distribution at the local level. And, to reach further afield, there is the buyer who not only pays the seller's price but consciously commits himself to purchase additional items exclusively from the seller because no other products will interface properly in the buyer's system. This latter example not only reflects the industrial-product situation in such fields as electronic test equipment and certain peripheral digital equipment but also describes a consumer-product situation as simple as that of the inexpensive razor with blades which have low compatibility with other blades on the market.

A moral suggests itself: Marketers need to inquire ingeniously into what elements of consideration, apart from price, may be available from the buyer.

The seller. To reverse matters, the seller often has a broad range of opportunity to bestow more consideration upon the buyer than merely the provision of the product or service which he offers. An obvious example involves hard goods which require installation or service or replacement parts. Buyers of consumer products are aware of the possible problems here—as is witnessed by their rejection of certain offerings by foreign suppliers because of questionable maintenance and repair service. We need only think of foreign cars in this connection. The same principal, however, applies to many industrial products.

Surprisingly, there are industrial buyers who are satisfied to specify a product, and who inquire into the availability of service and parts, but who fail to explore the cost and availability of these follow-on items. Whether or not such buyers represent a substantial number of potential customers for the industrial seller, he should be aware that his timely and economic provision of maintenance and parts is indeed one aspect of the consideration which accompanies delivery of the product itself. He may or may not include maintenance in the initial package, but he seemingly would be well advised—himself—to confront the eventual need for service and repair in structuring his pricing.

A manufacturer of underwater sound equipment for commercial fishermen once offered a lower-cost depth sounder to the pleasure-boat market. The potential buyers were sportsmen who, it was hoped, would use their discretionary income for this purchase. The high cost of maintaining and repairing equipment of this sort was well known. So, in recognition of the package nature of the consideration—comprising equipment, installation, and maintenance service—the seller wisely increased the price of his unit sufficiently to permit an attractive offer of flat-rate cost installation and, thereafter, a maximum ceiling which his billing for service would not exceed, whatever the character of the equipment breakdown might be. In this way, he captured a major share of the market.

ELASTICITIES OF DEMAND

The foregoing case of the electronics manufacturer hardly begins to tap the full range of possibilities available to sellers who take fair advantage of opportunities to bestow valuable nonfinancial consideration upon buyers.

It is useful to recall that today's generation of marketing people was educated to a free-and-open-competition model of economics during its secondary-school and college years. Part of this training involved the concept of "price elasticity of demand." In essence, this doctrine holds that, when price is altered to a slight extent and the responsive volume changes appreciably, the resulting phenomenon is characterized as "high price elasticity." Alternatively, if price is altered a great deal and the responsive volume changes very little, the resulting phenomenon is characterized as "low price elasticity." We suggest that in contemporary marketing the concept of elasticity of demand, as such, has lost relevance in some respects and gained relevance in others.

Today's marketing executives are ordinarily not dealing with a "free and open market." *Laissez-faire* was a dead issue in the United States prior to 1900. Instead, most markets are oligopolistic; they are referred to as containing the "Big Four, the Little Nine, and 41 'cats and dogs.'" Whether this kind of market is the result of legal observance of the natural laws of economics or some sinister nonverbal avoidance of the antitrust laws is quite beside the point of this commentary. The fact is that, notwithstanding the academics of pricing theory, sellers must observe the system in which they operate (be it an oligopoly or some other variant), appraise its competitive restraints, and rationally structure their consideration in a manner which will optimize their competitive stance.

This is not done by structuring price alone. Nor is it done by merely observing the classical doctrines of price elasticity. Instead, it requires the sort of marketing alchemy which considers not only price elasticity but also the other elasticities of demand. And these involve installation, service, advertising, styling, packaging, special promotions, and whatever else proves to be a valuable nonfinancial consideration in the exclusive discretion of the prospective buyer.

As a special illustration, consider the situation of the seller who contemplates cutting his price. In effect, he is offering the customer the additional consideration of retaining some of the customer's purchase money. The amount of this retainer represents the seller's investment in obtaining additional volume. However, a more sophisticated seller will question whether permitting the prospective buyer to retain purchase money to this extent is the wisest manner in which the seller can make this investment. Perhaps the seller can achieve even greater success by holding his product's price at its present level and investing, on his own behalf, a like amount of money in repackaging it, in heavier advertising, or in any number of other ways available to ingenious marketing executives. "Advertising elasticity of demand" or "packaging elasticity of demand," as examples, might prove better vehicles for the achievement of additional volume or share of market than the classical "price elasticity of demand."

ETHICAL ASPECTS OF PRICING

There is still another factor which must concern marketers, particularly those who distribute consumer products. This involves the ethical concept of "fair price," together with our cultural inheritance of theological overtones surrounding the adjective "fair."

It is possible for a group of competitive marketers individually and unilaterally to emphasize nonfinancial factors in their competition to a point where, as a group, they are laid open to the allegation that their several prices are unconscionably high and can be deemed "unfair" by commonly accepted social norms. This sort of allegation is popularly leveled against the manufacturers of breakfast cereals, the manufacturers of household detergents, and the manufacturers of prescription drug products. We need not pass judgment here upon the virtue of these allegations; it is enough merely to observe their existence. They are by no means confined to the three groups we have cited.

But suppose, for the purposes of discussion, that such an allegation is factual. We will then be dealing with a situation where, instead of paying scant attention to nonfinancial factors in pricing, we will have moved in the opposite direction to the point where price itself has gone beyond reasonable bounds. Through all this we will still be hard-pressed if asked how we might have counseled any one of the competitors, in the course of their competition, as to how he might avoid becoming a party to an "unfair" practice. Similarly, it will be difficult to make reasonable suggestions to the competitors as to how the group might proceed to re-establish an acceptable balance between price and nonprice factors.

It would be dangerous for such competitors, as a group, to act in concert because of the consequent liability under our antitrust laws. Therefore, it can be reasoned that those competitors who have had the marketing power to bring their industry into a nonprice competition model have also had the concomitant responsibility, socially and ethically, to temper their actions so as not to violate an implicit public trust. Where this responsibility is lacking, the end result can only be the "intrusion" of the government by way of regulation. Note the impact upon automobile marketing of the latest demands for product safety, the impact upon the food industry of recent legislation governing packaging and labeling, and the new legal requirements designed to promote public understanding of the lending rates imposed by finance companies.

There can be no doubt that the indefinable limits of "fair play" affect the latitude of a seller's right to structure his consideration. Let the doubtful reader consider the impact of Medicare upon the future free-pricing practices of physicians. Or the recent ado at the federal level over the protection of consumers. Or finally, and with more difficulty, let him analyze critically the interlineal suggestions for the future to be found in the antitrust decisions of our U.S. Supreme Court during recent years.

If, as so many aver, marketing is a profession, the marketing executives are like other professionals in having special social responsibilities which are made manifest in such important functions as pricing. It can even be suggested, controversially, that this professional responsibility transcends the top marketing executive's duty to be blindly obedient to the will of nonmarketing managers in his hierarchy. The penalty for violating the social ethic is evident.

More About Method: Variable or Marginal-Income Pricing

Douglas P. Gould

T HERE WAS A TIME, NOT LONG AGO, WHEN A DISCUSSION OF THE PROS AND CONS of variable pricing was a sure invitation to honest controversy. The rapid and widespread acceptance in recent years of the basic principles of break-even accounting as a most necessary premise in decision making, planning, and control has forced the acceptance of variable costing and pricing largely as a matter of practical logic.

A system of pricing predicated in the individual instance only on recognition of so-called variable or incremental costs once was felt by nonusers to be incomplete, misleading, and a false justification for cut prices. These views of course were offered chiefly in defense of traditional pricing and costing theory with little regard for the weaknesses of the timeworn basic concepts in managing the business. This chapter, then, will devote itself to

DOUGLAS P. GOULD is Vice President, Trundle Consultants Inc., in Cleveland, Ohio.

an exploration of the logic of the variable-cost pricing philosophy, to several key applications of the principle, and to the pricing technique itself.

THE MECHANICS OF PROFIT

Understanding the logic of variable pricing depends first on understanding the true mechanics of profit. While there are many ways of explaining the principles of profit development, a simple exercise involving the plotting of a scatter diagram of sales and profits before taxes on a periodic or monthly basis may be most easily understood. This we find in Exhibit 1.

Assuming, for the moment, no change in inventory from period to period, we see an obvious relationship between volume and pretax profit. A trend line drawn through the scatter by inspection, as in Exhibit 2, produces several findings of interest to a manager.

1. There is a point of no profit and no loss, a breakeven point.
2. With *no* sales, a predictable level of maximum loss is revealed.
3. The maximum loss is the amount of time costs, period costs, or fixed costs existing in the operation.
4. The relationship of volume and profit is predictable.
5. Profit develops when some incremental element in the sales dollar, across a sufficient number of sales dollars, totals enough to pay all the fixed costs—and then some.
6. Profit is a function of a company, not a product. For example, a 10-percent-profit *product* makes little sense if the *company* is operating below its breakeven point.
7. The rate at which the fixed costs, period costs, or time costs are liquidated depends on the line slope, which in the scatter diagram represents the difference between all out-of-pocket or variable costs and the total sales dollars.
8. This difference or increment is called "marginal income" or "profit contribution." It is *not* profit.
9. The average slope, or average marginal-income rate, existing for a given company is a function of all the variable costs and prices found in that company's marketing mix and product mix.
10. It is possible to find the marginal income or profit contribution for any product, from any marketing alternative, for any existing or proposed price. This is the source-of-profit figure so widely sought and so seldom found.

EXHIBIT 1

Scatter Diagram: Monthly Sales vs. Profit
(Before Taxes)

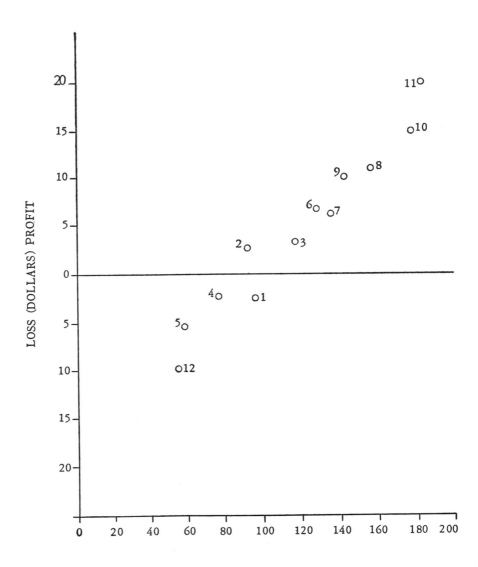

SALES VOLUME (DOLLARS)

EXHIBIT 2

Scatter Diagram: Monthly Sales vs. Profit
(Before Taxes)

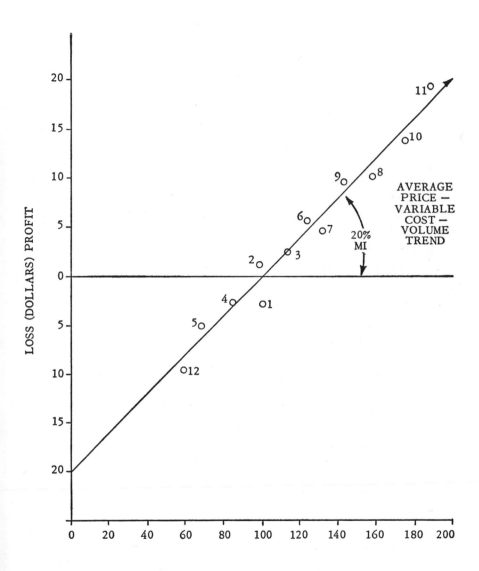

SALES VOLUME (DOLLARS)

11. Each individual price contributes positive or negative marginal income, actual or planned, determining the extent to which two of the three basic methods of profit development will be effective.
   a. Volume increase containing marginal income.
   b. Higher marginal income *rate,* from—
      (1) Higher price.
      (2) Lower variable costs.
      (3) Better product mix.
12. Fixed costs exist independently of unit price. Profit is created by attracting sufficient marginal-income dollars to liquidate the time or fixed costs—and then some.

As a concluding note on the origin of profit, management must have a consistent, realistic way of projecting the effect of greater or lesser volumes, at higher or lower prices, and from fixed-cost bases of varying levels. Clear separation of period or fixed costs from activity, incremental, out-of-pocket, direct, or variable costs becomes a necessity where conditions are subject to change. The separate factors affecting profit must be capable of separate analysis and treatment. "Horse apple," nonprojectable, or "mixed" costs are avoided in variable or incremental pricing.

DEVELOPING A PROPOSED PRICE

By using variable or marginal-income pricing, the effect on profit of any actual or proposed price can be determined quickly, easily, accurately, and consistently. A plan for pricing which will not readily indicate the profit effect, to the company, of a proposed price is unsuitable as a management method. The pricing method that is truly consistent with the actual mechanics of profit is variable or marginal-income pricing.

A proposed price is developed from known variable costs by the following method, predicated on three essential bits of knowledge:

1. The applicable *variable* burden rate or rates expressed in terms of direct labor dollars, hours, or some other suitable base.
2. The other items of variable cost peculiar to this product, manufactured and sold in this way to a customer in the area or areas concerned.
3. The required "par," or overall marginal-income percentage, re-

quired by the profit plan. This is dictated by company fixed-cost levels and return-on-investment objectives.

For example:

1. Determine variable costs per unit:

Material (in product)	$10.00
Direct labor	4.00
Variable manufacturing overhead at 150% of direct labor	6.00
Package	.50
Absorbed freight	1.00
Manufacturing and distribution: total known variables	$21.50

2. Determine selling and administrative variables as a percentage of unknown selling price—say, 10%.
3. Determine required marginal income—say, 30%.

Then:

$$\frac{\$21.50}{1.00 - (.30 + .10)} = \frac{\$21.50}{.60} = \$35.83 \text{ selling price}$$

The resultant price will cover all anticipated variable costs and will contain marginal income amounting to 30 percent of sales—or, in this case, $10.75 per unit. If the profit-plan requirement is 30 percent at forecast volume, this or better will be the price objective.

The price at which no contribution to fixed expense and profit is realized will be:

$$\frac{\$21.50}{1.00 - .10} = \frac{\$21.50}{.90} = \$23.88$$

Any sale below this figure will result in an out-of-pocket loss—or a negative marginal income.

In establishing price patterns, it is well to identify the extremes, and it is most important to identify any and all specific cost elements such as pack-

EXHIBIT 3

Comparative Price Lines at Different MI Rates
(New Program)

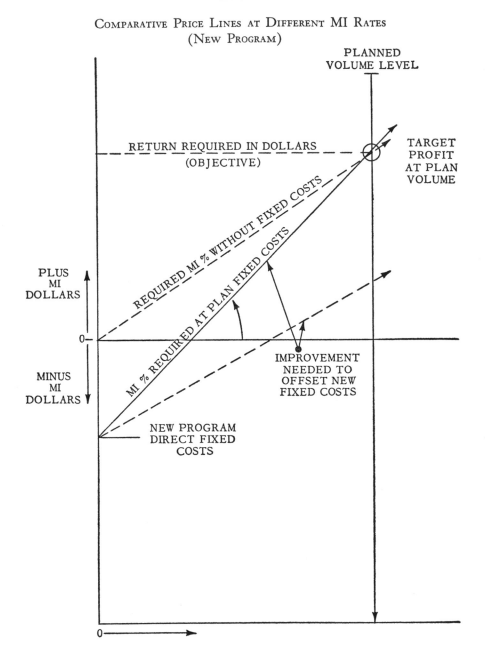

SALES VOLUME (DOLLARS)

age, printing, interleaving, colors, modifications, commissions, absorbed freight, and the like that are associated with this sale and identified as true variable costs. These costs literally can be anything that adds measurably to the cost of *each* unit. New costs, like tooling, special engineering, and added equipment, which result from the new volume are in reality *additions* to fixed costs. As such, they are a part of the price decision, but they are a component of actual price only in determining the level of marginal income required to offset them and still meet plan requirements. (See Exhibit 3.)

EVALUATING AN EXISTING PRICE

Variable or marginal-income pricing is in fact used (1) to determine, as shown, the proposed price for a new product (or to fix the price stated in a contract or a bid) and (2) to analyze one's own or a competitor's existing price.

The problems of pricing new products or services, or of bidding on new work or on existing services with new customers, respond well to the variable costing or marginal-income logic. However, a problem which lends itself particularly well to the technique, and which recurs frequently, concerns the evaluation of an existing price from the standpoint of the profit contribution or marginal-income dollars which it provides or can provide at various volumes.

The real dollar contribution to fixed expense and profit resulting from the existing or planned price is identified in terms of a single unit or a quantity of units. Such units may be items, gallons, pounds, loads, tons, yards, or whatever. In the previous case, assume the existence of a realized price of $30.00 per unit in lots of 5 or less; $28.00 for lots of 5 to 20; and $25.00 each for quantities of 20 to 50. The variable cost per unit produced and sold in quantity is $23.88. The comparative yields of these prices will be:

Quantity	Price Each	$ MI/Unit	$ MI on Quantity	Units to Produce $100 MI	MI %
5	$30	$6.12	$30.60	16.3	20.4
20	$28	$4.12	$82.40	24.3	14.7
50	$25	$1.12	$56.00	89.2	4.5

Thus an existing price, whether one's own or a competitor's, is analyzed by relating all known or presumed variable costs to it and determining the difference. This difference is the marginal income at that price. It should be noted that in evaluating existing prices, *no* fixed burdens are considered other than those peculiar direct fixed costs, existing by reason of the program under investigation, which would drop if the program were eliminated.

In brief, six steps are required in reviewing the adequacy or inadequacy of an existing price:

1. Determination of the actual realized net price.
2. Determination of the applicable variable burden rate or rates.
3. Determination of the actual direct labor and direct material involved—or the standard labor and material plus variances and any other variables such as freight and commissions.
4. Determination of the unit and dollar sales volume (*a*) which is achieved and (*b*) which it is felt should be achievable at the price.
5. Determination of the relationship of the MI percentage for the product or service to that for the overall company or division.
6. Identification of any direct fixed costs caused by and peculiar to the situation at hand.

For example:

Published "book" price per unit		$20.00
Invoice 12786: "realized" price per unit		$17.00
Per unit cost		
Direct labor	$4.75	
Direct material	5.10	
Variable manufacturing		
burden at 100%		
direct labor	4.75	
Variable selling and		
administrative expense		
at 5% sales	1.00	
Freight (paid by us)	.80	
	——	
		$16.40
		——

Actual unit marginal income $ .60

$$\frac{\$.60}{\$17.00} = 3.53\%$$

Planned unit marginal income $ 3.60

$$\frac{\$3.60}{\$20.00} = 18.0\%$$

This example points up the common area of MI loss through casual price reductions. To achieve the same marginal income effect in dollars at the $17.00 invoice price as would be obtained at the planned $20.00 price, it would be necessary to sell six times as many units at the lower price as at the planned price. For instance:

(1) Actual $ MI per unit: $ .60
(2) Planned $ MI per unit: $3.60

$$\frac{Planned \quad \$3.60}{Actual \quad \$\ .60} = 6 \text{ (volume factor)}$$

Clearly, then, variable-cost analysis is a practical prelude to price determination or modification. But it is more than that. It provides the courage to "back off," to refuse business, to withdraw from territories, to drop products—courage which comes from the informed realization that such actions in many cases will cause a measurable, predictable increase in profit or a decrease in loss. Indeed, to establish a proper direction for the marketing effort and to pinpoint the sources of important profit contribution or, conversely, out-of-pocket loss, management is *forced* to review periodically the source and extent of the marginal-income dollars it receives.

PRICING "PAR"

Strangely, the question most often asked in pricing analysis is not, "What price will get this business?" but, "What is the price pattern we should work to?"

In a "pure" situation or a "clean" example, the basic price level, "par," or pricing formula for any company is determined by four factors:

1. Fixed expense level.
2. Dollars of return required before taxes.

3. Capacity in units, hours, dollars, or other measure.
4. Available market at a price.

A breakeven chart (Exhibit 4) reveals the analysis required. For a given level of fixed cost, a given capacity, and a given ROI objective, only one marginal-income rate will be satisfactory: that shown by Line AB. As a profit-plan price line, this provides the par base and the necessary frame of reference for pricing decisions. Its slope is determined by dividing fixed cost (A) by the breakeven point (C).

The par base may be expressed in "MI $/Hour" where process equipment or other time-limiting facilities are involved. We may speak, for example, of loom-hours or machine-hours. At capacity, expressed in hours, we wish to earn, say, $100,000 before taxes. What is the price criterion? Fixed expense is $400,000; $100,000 is the required pretax return; capacity (for two shifts) is 32,000 hours. The MI $/Hour required at par to meet plan is thus:

$$\frac{\$400,000 + \$100,000}{32,000} = \frac{\$500,000}{32,000} = \$15.63$$

Development of the price requirement in terms of marginal income "per hour" as opposed to "per dollar" permits much greater accuracy in selection of product and customers, particularly in capacity situations, and provides different and more realistic objectives in those industries where the measure is applicable.

THE "RIGHT" QUESTIONS

In attempting to achieve a realistic approach to pricing a product, job, service, or line, other questions are often raised:

1. What would the profit be on this product at the proposed price?
2. What is the total cost of this product?
3. How much volume will it take to cover the cost of a new salesman out of our profit?
4. At this price and quantity would we over- or underabsorb our burden?

Unfortunately, while questions like these are common, they contribute only confusion to the pricing problem. In attempting to determine and evaluate

EXHIBIT 4

DETERMINATION OF THE "PAR" PRICE
LINE TO SATISFY OTHER FIXED
ELEMENTS OF PROFIT PLAN

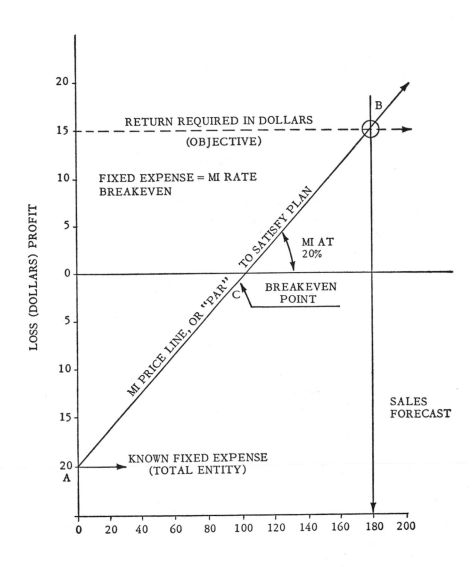

the effectiveness, real or probable, of a price, there are only six fundamental questions which must be asked. These are:

1. What is the marginal income per unit, in dollars and percent, at the price?
2. How many units can we sell at that price? How much MI will result?
3. What new fixed costs must be added, if any, in connection with the adoption of this price?
4. Did we include *all* the variable costs pertinent to this situation in our estimate?
5. How does this MI rate compare with our profit-plan rate?
6. What kind of return on investment does this price provide?

With a basic knowledge of fixed and variable costs, and some relevant knowledge of the probable market acceptance of the product, these meaningful questions can be answered. Without a knowledge of fixed and variable costs, including the nature of the several burden accounts, they cannot be answered precisely.

Return on direct investment. For example, by knowing the marginal income resulting from a given price and variable-cost situation, plus the inventory-turnover rate, the comparative return on variable investment (that is, the variable cost of average inventory versus the number of margins "sold" or obtained) can be directly determined. Assume that, for Product *A*, MI equals 25 percent and variable costs equal 75 percent of sales price. The average inventory is 2.6 weeks' supply; therefore, the rate of turnover is 20. Thus:

$$\frac{\text{MI (as decimal)} \times \text{rate of turn}}{\text{Variable cost (as decimal) of average inventory}} = \text{return on variable investment}$$

$$\frac{.25}{.75} \times 20 = \frac{5.00}{.75} = 6.67 \text{ return per direct dollar invested}$$

An illustration of the comparative measurements is to be found in the table that follows:

Turnover Rate	Weeks of Supply in Inventory	MI Percentages *				
		21	22	23	24	25
		Return per Direct Dollar Invested				
20.0	2.6	5.32	5.64	5.97	6.32	6.67
19.3	2.7	5.12	5.43	5.75	6.08	6.42
18.6	2.8	4.94	5.24	5.55	5.86	6.19
17.9	2.9	4.77	5.06	5.36	5.66	5.98
17.3	3.0	4.61	4.89	5.18	5.47	5.78

* Usable, complete percentage tables are to be found in D'Anna, John P., *Inventory and Profit*, American Management Association, 1966.

Over a period of time, and within any company, these ROI figures on marginal income in a price related to variable costs are an excellent selective marketing index.

Price-volume decisions. Decisions are made daily affecting the marketing and product mix of any company. A sound knowledge of the industry pricing structure in terms of the usual level of marginal income or profit contribution provided by prices received has a major effect on all these decisions. A few representative instances drawn from manufacturing industries will serve to reveal the importance of knowing the percentage of marginal income in a price as obtained by extracting variable or incremental costs. The following figures are approximate, and significant deviations may occur within the averages.

Industry	% MI	Breakeven Effect of Adding $1,000 to Fixed Costs
Fowl processing	5.	+$20,000
Food (oils)	7.	+$14,286
Foundry	25.	+$ 4,000
Paint	30.	+$ 3,333
Stamping	33.	+$ 3,030
Instrument making	50.	+$ 2,000
Drugs	60.	+$ 1,666
Cosmetics	70.	+$ 1,428

It is imperative to know the change in volume required at given price levels to offset contemplated changes in fixed costs, whether they are additions or deductions. An example is the decision to add a salesman at a salary of $10,000 in any one of these industries. His breakeven volume will vary from $200,000 in one case to only $14,280 in another.

Product-group pricing. Analysis of market prices for products within product lines, or for groups of products that may be dissimilar in nature, often reveals useful areas of similarity. For purposes of review, comparison, and projection, such products may be grouped by application, market, territory, customer, channel of distribution, turnover rate, life-cycle stage, labor-material content, or extent of marketing function performed. The reasons for such determination of pricing similarity are varied, but development of a logical system of differences in prices to different customers or to the same customers is invariably an important consideration. To "guess right" on prices, it is useful to be able to project in a consistent fashion.

A case in point concerns the kind of price analysis that relates existing prices to the labor-material ratios of the several, possibly dissimilar line items. Thus:

| | Ratio of Material Cost to Direct Labor Cost in Product | | | | |
MI Rate	(A)	(B)	(C)	(D)	(E)
10%	6–1				
20%		4–1			
30%			2–1		
40%				1–1	
50%					1–3

While results vary in different markets and product lines, it becomes apparent that high material-low variable labor cost items tend to yield low MI rates. On the other hand, high variable labor-low material cost items tend to produce high MI rates. Numerous examples can be cited—as in commodity processing, food distribution, and certain assembly operations —where low MI rates may prevail. But, where extensive direct labor is applied to raw material, MI rates tend to be higher.

Variable-cost and price analysis, in short, is peculiarly adaptable as a tool for exploring the causes and extent of underlying price differences. Often, by knowing the actual or probable amounts and ratios of labor and materials a competitive market price can be predicted with reasonable accuracy.

Automation and pricing philosophy. Several multiplant operations which encourage price competition or open bidding among their divisions or subsidiaries as a means of insuring a "competitive" level of performance on work to be done for other divisions, or under contract, have made serious mistakes by using bid prices predicated on so-called "full" costs.

The difference is clearly illustrated by the bid performance of two plants: one, (*A*), old and depreciated; two, (*B*), new, automated, and operating under provision for rapid depreciation.

Case 1: "Full" cost (including fixed burdens)

(A)		(B)
$12	Labor	$10
30	Material	26
24	Overhead	34
$66	Manufacturing cost	$70

Case 2: Variable cost only

(A)		(B)
$12	Labor	$10
30	Material	26
12	Variable burden	8
$54	Manufacturing cost	$44

In Case 1, old Plant *A* gets the job on the basis of lower costs than new Plant *B*. The real effect of this action is revealed in Case 2. Plant *B,* with higher continuing fixed costs already in existence, but with lower variables, can put an additional $10 per unit of marginal income into the corporate fixed expense-profit pool. However, it is denied the opportunity owing to unrealistic pricing and costing practices.

Bid control. Many concerns are engaged in competitive bidding on contracts, proposals, jobs, or services of various types for industry, government, users, and large distributors. There is no fixed price schedule, but each situation requires a decision to bid or not to bid, a decision to bid in the manner and according to the terms specified or to bid in a different manner, and, in due course, a decision on the bid price.

In these situations it is most important that the company's pricing specialist or bid committee be fully aware of—

1. The fixed costs for the period.
2. Any new fixed costs to be generated by the bid.

3. All variable costs involved in the satisfaction of the proposed contract.
4. The existing situation relative to in-house marginal income for this period and the ability to deliver during the periods specified by the proposal.
5. Prior variable costs and prior bid prices on the same or similar work, successful and unsuccessful.

It is at this point that the peculiar advantage of variable or marginal-income pricing and costing becomes most evident in terms of "knowing where you are."

By completing an analysis sheet similar to that shown as Exhibit 5, all factors of variable and *new* fixed costs are identified. The absolute base price is thus available. This is the price represented by the variable cost, with *no* marginal income. To sell below that price is to court an immediate out-of-pocket loss. Something above that figure is obviously required. The MI yield of several proposed prices is scanned; then, on the basis of market knowledge, profit plan, and in-house marginal income in the proposed delivery periods, a realistic bid price is developed and approved.

At this point, all factors being favorable, the decision to bid is made. A simple 3 x 5 card which is completed shows an identifying proposal number, the marginal-income dollars represented by the bid, and the approximate delivery period when those dollars will be realized if the bid is accepted. Most concerns have been able to predict, from experience, the approximate percentage of bids they will obtain on proposals. By noting the continuing value in marginal income on the open-bid board, applying the "success percentage," and considering the MI value of successful bids already obtained, they can achieve a good measure of available MI dollars relative to fixed expense and profit needs for the period in question. This situation report, maintained on a period and cumulative basis, can dictate the need to (1) reduce price to insure enough MI to at least pay fixed expenses, (2) hold out or bid at a higher MI where fixed expenses are already covered or the job is not particularly desirable, (3) price the bid so as to insure the best chance of obtaining it if fixed expenses are largely covered but open capacity exists, or (4) take such other appropriate action as subcontracting or overtime production.

Many variations on this form of control are possible and in use. The key advantage is, however, awareness at all times of the impact of any price cut,

EXHIBIT 5

Bid Analysis

Customer
Bid No.
Quantity

Contract $ MI at Bid Price — Total	% by Month (est.)		
	1	2	3
	4	5	6

Part No. _____
Description _____
Submitted by _____
Date _____
Delivery by _____
Start _____
End _____

Analysis of Direct Labor

Category	Hours	Rate/ Hour	Unit Cost	Ext.
Manufacturing				
Dept. A				
Dept. B				
Dept. C				
Dept. D				
Total Mfg. Labor $				
Var. O'Head @___% D.L.A				
Var. O'Head @___% D.L.B				
Var. O'Head @___% D.L.C				
Var. O'Head @___% D.L.D				
Total				
Engineering F | V				
Project				
Design				
Test				
Draft & Check				
Total				
Var. O'Head @___% Total				
Tooling				
Total				
Other D. L. (Specify)				
Other Var. Overhead @___% .D.L.				
Total				
Total Direct Labor				
Total Var. O'Head				

Variable-Cost Analysis

	$	$
Direct Labor (M&E)		
Projected Labor Increase ___%		
Total Direct Labor		
Var. O'Head (Total)		
Base Material		
Subcontract Material		
Package Material		
Total Material		
Other Variable Cost (Mfg.)		
Travel		
Living		
———		
———		
Total		
Estimated G&A & ___%		
Commission @ ___%		
Freight from ___ to ___		
Total Var. Cost		$
New or Added Fixed Costs		

Unit Price		Approved
@ 20% MI	$	
@ 25% MI	$	
@ 30% MI	$	
@ 35% MI	$	
@ __% MI	$	

or any individual bid, in terms of planned-profit and fixed-cost requirements. Such control encourages intelligent, courageous, and informed pricing in accordance with need.

THE "UNINFORMED" COMPETITOR

In almost every type of business and industry there are price leaders and
price followers. Frequently they change places. In both groups there are informed competitors and uninformed competitors. To judge by the variations in pricing policy encountered in the market, it is often difficult to tell
the one from the other.

A common complaint is that Competitor *A,* for example, is selling
"below cost." It is not at all unusual to encounter competitors who are in
the market aggressively, with prices well under those of reasonably well-es-
tablished firms that rely on a "full" standard cost-price method—including
provision for "profit" in the job or product. Such prices may constitute dis-
tress pricing or may, in fact, reflect a very realistic insight into profit-
volume economics.

An example involving a $60.00 market price may be revealing. Case 1
involves the application of full overheads in the analysis, with fixed expense
allocated to product on whatever arbitrary base is selected. Case 2 reflects
planned variable-pricing strategy.

Case 1: "Full" costs

$10.00	Direct labor
30.00	Direct material
20.00	Full manufacturing burden (200% of direct labor)
6.00	Selling and administrative expense at 10% of selling price
(6.00)	Loss at 10%
$60.00	Price

Case 2: MI or variable-cost price

$10.00	Direct labor
30.00	Direct material
10.00	*Variable* manufacturing burden (100% of direct labor)
2.50	*Variable* selling and administrative expense
7.50	MI dollar contribution
$60.00	

In the first case, the sale would appear to produce a 10 percent loss. In the second case, the real fact is apparent that at comparable *variable* costs, as known by the supplier, a profit contribution or marginal income of $7.50, or 12.5 percent, results. Without knowledge of this fact and thorough analysis of burdens to determine their fixed or variable components, the first supplier could easily abandon a market to the second in order to avoid a fictitious loss.

In cases of this sort, the "uninformed competitor" is the one who is not in a position to put himself accurately, for analysis purposes, on the same cost level as his competitor—who may, in fact, be a shortline, "alley shop" low-overhead operator.

Marginal-income and variable-cost analysis presents the real facts. It is conceivable that the decision to abandon a market, for example, will remain the same. It will not, however, be based on incorrect pricing data.

+ + +

The objective of a good pricing policy is to insure that the company's products or services are sold at prices high enough to satisfy the company's profit requirements. In some cases those prices should encourage volume sales; in others they should exploit the advantages of selective selling; in still others they should be the direct reflection of an aggressive competitive stance. In any case, capacity, volume, variable costs, fixed costs, and investment are intermingled as influences on price. Variable pricing and related variable costing provide, in understandable fashion, a key to the *why* of pricing, its timing, and its effect. Granted, a price must be high enough, but difficulty often is experienced in defining "high enough." With marginal-income or variable pricing, however, this definition is readily made in each instance. And "high enough" prices are one hallmark of good management.

The objective of a price is to provide marginal-income dollars. A price which fails in this elementary respect is obviously unsuitable. A price must provide *enough* marginal-income dollars, and this is why volume, fixed costs, and variable costs must become integral but separate parts of the pricing equation. The effect of each must be identified for proper analysis.

Pricing by Distribution Method

I. The Wholesale Level

Fred M. Truett

IN SELLING TO WHOLESALERS, DISTRIBUTORS, OR JOBBERS, ONE OF TWO TYPES OF prices generally is quoted: (1) list or (2) net. *List* price begins with the retail price and works backward. Normally, the retailer is allowed a discount of 20 to 40 percent. After this there is a discount of 10 to 25 percent for the wholesale distributor. If, for example, the retail discount is 40 percent and the wholesale 16⅔ percent, the manufacturer is selling 50 percent of list. *Net* price means exactly that. The manufacturer sells to his distributors at a net price, and they set their own resale prices.

Whichever method of pricing is used, the manufacturer must be concerned with the retail price. Is it one that the consumer will pay? Does it offer the retailer an acceptable profit? Is the retail price competitive with those of similar products? And the wholesaler must be considered—he too must have an acceptable profit. Distributors, whether retail or wholesale, have little interest in pushing merchandise when the profit structure is inadequate.

FRED M. TRUETT is Chairman of the Board, Southwestern Drug Corporation, Dallas, Texas.

For his own benefit the manufacturer normally wants his product priced at retail on a par with competitive products. Theoretically, the list price is the retail price—and it is one that tests have shown the consumer is willing to pay. Actually, though, the retail price may be cut well below list. And, when the manufacturer sells at net, he loses some of his control over the retail price. Legally he has none, but the power of suggestion—plus the desire to make a profit—leans heavily in favor of list, a suggested price to the consumer.

PROBLEMS SHARED BY MOST WHOLESALERS

What pricing problems do distributors have? To find out at first hand, let us look at eight types of wholesalers: those dealing with drugs, dry goods, food, hardware, jewelry, liquor, tobacco, and toiletries. All eight of these wholesale industries appear to have three difficulties in common today that materially affect their pricing:

1. Direct selling by manufacturers.
2. Strong competition from other sources.
3. The profit squeeze.

The one type of wholesaler that seems least affected by these difficulties is the rack jobber, a specialized operator handling drugs and toiletries. Since his customers can be considered "captive," the rack jobber has little competition, if any, but he may very well have pricing problems. A customer may demand, say, that a group of items carry a heavy price cut, which has an adverse effect on the jobber's profit from that particular retailer. Then, if there are other rackers operating in the same area, pricing problems can come from two directions: First, a competitor may offer a greater discount to the retailer in an attempt to take away the business. Second, retailers served by other rack jobbers may start a price war, thus forcing a drop in prices and profits all along the line.

Like other wholesalers, the rack jobber feels the same sort of profit squeeze from inflationary factors. But his customers prefer service to price. He is, therefore, virtually immune to competition from direct-selling manufacturers—which, of all the pricing problems that wholesalers face, is the most difficult to combat.

Often, nowadays, the manufacturer skims the cream from a market. He sells to a selected group of the larger retailers and chains at or close to the same price he charges wholesalers, and in this way he minimizes the volume that wholesalers can do on his line. They are left with the smaller accounts and, naturally, a smaller volume. To meet this direct-selling threat, the wholesaler must sell at or near cost, with an adverse effect on his profits.

Discount stores are another strong factor in the competition with which the wholesaler must cope as he sets his prices. Buying in large quantities, they tend to get better prices than the wholesaler. Also, they are highly successful in gaining discounts and allowances, for one reason or another, which bring their costs still lower. They can really create havoc with their price advantage.

For early bookings on lawn mowers a hardware wholesaler can ordinarily get an extra 5 percent discount. To get early orders, however, he passes on all or part of the extra discount. In one typical case the wholesaler's salesman performed well, selling 1,500 mowers at a price of $35.22—a cut under the normal price of $37.85. But the manufacturer sold the same lawn mower to a discount store in the same area at a price which permitted the discounter to advertise the item at $33.79 retail. Frequently, under such circumstances (which are not at all unusual), wholesalers reluctantly drop a line because independent retailers refuse to buy the brand.

Wholesalers have problems, moreover, because of the multiple channels through which consumer goods are now distributed. This trend is increasing, not decreasing, and pricing definitely feels the impact of the marketing maneuvers occasioned by what we might term the distribution upheaval. To illustrate: Wholesalers handling photo film suddenly find themselves greatly underpriced by film developers who use a low price on film (at or near cost) as bait to get more developing business.

And, with all these comparatively new and varied forms of competition making it tough for the wholesaler, he still must face and try to outwit his familiar rivals: other wholesalers. In the scramble for volume, these normal competitors may have been engaging in a variety of more or less complex forms of discounting—both on and under the table. They are tough opponents, well versed in all phases of their industry.

Finally, along with all businessmen, wholesalers are suffering from the profit squeeze caused by inflation, taxes, higher labor costs, inefficiencies, and the like. When wholesalers deal primarily in merchandise with fixed list prices, they lack flexibility; the prices are too well known or too easily checked. Even net-price items which are everyday fast sellers offer no opportunity for increased profit.

Frequently the wholesaler receives a double dose of pressure: At the same time he is feeling the profit squeeze, so are his suppliers. But the manufacturers can do something to alleviate their troubles—such as reducing the wholesaler's discount. Against such action the wholesaler is basically defenseless.

ADAPTING TO THE NEW ORDER

There are, however, solutions to the wholesaler's dilemma. First of all, he must accept conditions as they are and resolve to seek mass volume at lower margins. This decision has confronted countless wholesalers in countless industries. In reducing prices to be competitive, they of course have found it necessary to make economies as well, to lower their operating costs to offset the drop in gross profit. The wholesalers who have done this and survived (and there are many) have become infinitely stronger.

Strangely, in this pandemonium of price wars, some wholesalers are building on a foundation of quality and service—and are succeeding handsomely, with a beneficial effect on both prices and profits. They are buying and selling better grades of merchandise. They are encountering a minimum of competition and practically no price cutting. And with this upgrading of merchandise wholesalers are striving diligently to give their retail accounts much better service. Many are working with retailers to help them buy more wisely, get more turnover, and make greater profits. In short, wholesalers have intelligently analyzed the conditions that face them and acted accordingly. They have adapted to the new order.

Failure to do this in the 1950's almost wiped out the food wholesaler. Today he is in an enviable position of strength, often operating under two different types of food distribution.

Quality in the right place at the right time. The first of the two types is of recent vintage but growing fast: hotel and institutional food service. Its customers, who prepare food for resale, include hotels, motels, restaurants, cafeterias, hospitals, caterers, and so on. This form of food wholesaling represents the best traditions of the past; it is truly old-fashioned, for it is wholly based on quality and service.

The buyer of institutional foods is primarily interested in consistent quality delivered to the right place at the right time. To a large extent items are sold (and priced) by controlled portion. A can of green peas may provide 12 servings; one of another brand, at relatively the same price, as many as 15. The stress is on the cost per serving without sacrifice of quality.

More and more Americans are "eating out." Whatever the reason may be—the servant problem or more housewives working—this is a growing trend. And it has enhanced the profit structure of the food wholesaler.

Return of the private label and house brand. The other side of the picture, the mass distribution of food products to retail food stores, is entirely different. Here we see a low-margin, high-volume business which is probably the most competitive of all wholesaling. High volume and rapid turnover are necessary for existence, much less profit. Most food wholesalers are happy to have a 0.5 percent of sales net after taxes. A net of 0.75 percent after taxes represents an unusually good return on investment.

Today pricing by the food wholesaler follows two patterns. The differential is caused by a shift from the proverbial way of doing business 15 or more years ago. At that time the bulk of sales was in national brands. Food wholesalers operated on a cost-plus price basis, the plus factor added to cost varying with the volume of the purchase and ranging from 3 to 6.5 percent. This pattern produced an average income of 4 to 4.5 percent of the selling price and normally resulted in a profit, before taxes, of 1 percent.

In the 1960's, private labels or house brands returned and food wholesalers began to see opportunities for added profit. This was to become a truly protected profit, but it could not operate on a phony cost-plus. Fairly quickly the pattern became one of low prices on national brands, and the recapture of profits on private labels, while still underselling national brands. Example: A well-known brand of coffee, heavily and consistently advertised from coast to coast, costs the food wholesaler 70 cents per pound. He charges his retailers this same 70 cents per pound. To recapture his profits, the wholesaler buys a coffee of comparable quality at 60 cents per pound and wholesales it at 63 cents.

What is actually happening today in the mass distribution of food is that the wholesaler is doing a large volume on national brands at margins that vary from the extremely small to no profit whatsoever. To make money, therefore, he must resort to making a sizable percentage of his sales in house brands. This he can do because of a radical change in consumer purchasing. Whereas, earlier, no one wanted private labels, today a large and growing percentage of consumers buy on price, not on brand name.

Most of these buyers are young and, perhaps, less sophisticated. Unlike the older generation of housewives, they did not have the experience, during World War II, of having to buy inferior products; they do not feel compelled to stick with national brands regardless of price. Moreover, the younger woman is skeptical of excessive advertising claims. Probably, however, the important factor in today's changed buying habits is young people's insatiable appetite for so many *things:* homes, diamonds, furs, yachts, autos, trips. When they find a chance to save—as by buying house brands in quantity—they do so, hoping their thriftiness will enable them to buy more of these things they want so badly.

Further protection for profit margins. In the 1950's the food wholesaler was essentially a distributor. Today he is primarily a procurer of quality private-label merchandise. He has even, when hard pressed to survive, ventured into the retail field, either opening his own chain of supermarkets or forming a voluntary chain of independent food stores. Thus the food wholesaler insures himself a large volume, protects his margins (even though they are low), and perpetuates the house brands on which he makes his profit.

Other industries are watching the food wholesaler carefully, thinking about following his lead. Notably in drugs, dry goods, and hardware—where wholesalers also are fighting a decline in profits—they are turning to private labels. Groups of wholesalers, relatively noncompetitive, are forming buying organizations for purchasing private-brand merchandise. Thus they are able to get lower prices on their combined purchases, undersell the price-cut national brands, and still make an acceptable profit. In a few instances wholesalers are acquiring franchise lines on which they can protect their price margins.

One wholesale industry which must operate with notoriously low margins is liquor. Most alcoholic beverages are sold on a net-price basis; discounts are rarely allowed. When a price concession is to be made to the retailer, it usually takes the form of so many dollars per case off—$2.00, $3.00, $5.00—depending on the number of cases bought. Normally, on such promotions, the distiller contributes all or the greater part of the allowance. Like the food wholesaler, the liquor wholesaler does a large volume; otherwise he would find it exceedingly difficult to net the small percentage he does.

The art of pricing alcoholic beverages makes the difference, in fact, between profit and loss. To set his price schedule, the wholesaler must determine what price the consumer will pay for a given item. Then, within the prescribed limit, he must provide an acceptable profit for the retailer and leave one for himself. This is a backward but effective approach to wholesale pricing.

In many states the wholesaler of alcoholic beverages distributes franchised lines and items and, technically, has no competition on his brands, but he has ample competition from other wholesalers offering comparable products. It is fortunate for him that consumers seem to tie quality and price together—a whiskey at $5.49 a fifth must be better than one at $4.89.

Indeed, the liquor wholesaler has a quirk of human nature going for him, and a great aid to pricing for profit it is. Certain fine liquor products are considered status symbols; they sell at relatively high prices, and sales tend to fall off sharply when retail prices are deeply cut. It is therefore possible to take a quality product (never a low-quality or inferior product), overprice it, promote it diligently, and build it into a top seller—at a long profit for both wholesaler and retailer. The status symbol that the host proudly pours may be scotch, bourbon, or gin, but one thing is certain: It is higher-priced than most competitive brands.

All wholesalers find that an aggressive sales force can be helpful. With such a selling group it is not necessary to meet the lowest prices; instead, prices can be set somewhere above the average low but well under the high. On the other hand, a mediocre sales force lacks the ability to outsell competition and must have low prices to get orders.

How the Manufacturer Can Help

The outlook for wholesalers is by no means a dark one, however harmful the effect of current pricing practices on profits. For the past century wholesalers have been beset with innumerable problems, but they have always been able to adapt to changing circumstances and overcome all difficulties. They will continue to offer their very vital services and to survive at a profitable level.

Manufacturers, however, might well be more sympathetic toward wholesalers' needs. To find themselves becoming distributors might be most unpleasant and costly in view of added labor requirements and inexperience in warehousing and other distribution areas. Far better to cooperate with the wholesalers, to take a sincere interest in their ability to make an acceptable profit.

For one thing, manufacturers might ask themselves whether the proliferation of product brands, sizes, and styles is really necessary and perhaps take steps to reduce any excess to normal. Too many of these product variations are brought on the market ostensibly to meet a demand but actually to fill up the pipeline and get added volume. From the wholesaler's standpoint they tend to magnify pricing problems and make it exceedingly difficult to stay competitive—profitably.

To aid their wholesalers, manufacturers should give careful consideration, also, to variable pricing. As an illustration, let us take a hypothetical manufacturer who produces and markets 100 items. Available data show that 12 of these items account for 70 percent of the company's volume, 26 items for 20 percent, and the remaining 62 items for 10 percent. The manufacturer's discount to wholesalers is 16⅔ percent on all items, without regard to turnover or profit possibilities. With variable pricing, however, the first group would remain at 16⅔ percent, the second group would be advanced to 20 percent, and the last group would be priced at 25 percent off list. This form of pricing is far more realistic than the straight discount across the board, which carries a penalty on all items except the fastest sellers.

A prolonged continuation of the present situation in wholesale pricing can be counted on to encourage still further recourse to such devices as private-label merchandise. This is inevitable; to survive, certainly to grow, wholesalers *must* make satisfactory profits. If forced, they will seek more and more to recoup their losses on national brands. It is a matter of record that house brands can become regional brands, as strong as the heavily advertised national brands. They may eventually outdistance their competitors on a countrywide basis and be national brands themselves; for without the benefit of in-store display, or where national brands and less expensive house brands are displayed and price-compared, advertising has been known to lose its force.

An inadequate profit structure for the distributor may enhance the manufacturer's profits for a time, but there may come a day when the manufacturer's products have been replaced. If consumer preference and market position are to be maintained, the profit requirements of both wholesalers and retailers must be taken into account.

II. *The Retail Level*

Peter G. Scotese

Department store pricing is highly flexible. It is influenced by gross margin and turnover objectives as well as attributable direct and indirect expenses and certain merchandising considerations. It would seem that these factors ought also to influence pricing for supermarkets, chains and mail order houses, discount operations, and other forms of retailing.

In some fields—for example, textile manufacturing—pricing decisions do not have the same complexities. In most cases, the pricing variables to be considered are more clearly defined. In the retail business, however, there are literally hundreds of buyers making thousands of pricing decisions in a given organization over a period of a year—this in contrast to the handful of top-level executives or product managers making relatively few such decisions over the same length of time in most manufacturing businesses.

Influences on Retail Price

Let us first outline those factors which should be considered before a retailer makes a pricing decision.

PETER G. SCOTESE is Chairman of the Boston Store in Milwaukee, Wisconsin (a division of Federated Department Stores, Inc.). His earlier background was largely in textile manufacturing.

GROSS MARGIN

The gross margin objective exerts the greatest influence on pricing. Stated very simply, gross margin is what is left from the markup dollar after certain specified costs have been deducted. The gross margin dollar must be planned to cover direct and indirect expense and leave a margin of profit. Retail managements generally look upon gross margin objectives as more meaningful than markup objectives.

Specifically, gross margin is the difference between the retail net sales and the six factors of unit cost (including transportation and subtracting cash discounts), markdowns, shortages, employee discounts, workroom costs, and other costs of sales. These elements may be defined in the following way:

> *Unit cost.* The base cost of a selling unit, as shown on the vendor's or manufacturer's invoice.
>
> *Transportation.* The cost of transporting goods from supplier to store.
>
> *Cash discounts.* Terms granted by vendor for paying invoice within a specific time period.
>
> *Markdowns.* Reductions in original retail price because of buying mistakes, promotions, soilage, damage, and the like.
>
> *Inventory shortages.* Reduction in the value of owned inventory at retail price due to theft or improper record keeping, causing physical inventory to be less than book inventory. This figure can vary significantly from year to year and is unusually high in percentage and dollars among self-service forms of retailing such as supermarkets and discount department stores.
>
> *Employee discounts.* Reductions from retail prices of merchandise due to allowances given employees on certain kinds of merchandise for personal use.
>
> *Workroom costs.* Includes costs of transforming merchandise into usable condition after sale has been made. For example: alterations, installation costs, and furniture finishing.
>
> *Other costs of sales.* Represents the expense of placing merchandise in salable condition before offering for sale. Such charges include setup and repair, pressing, replacement of belts, buttons, and so on, and other miscellaneous expenses.

These cost factors which affect gross margin are influenced in varying degrees by the buyer. Whereas he has very little influence on workroom and other costs of sales, his buying judgment significantly influences the mark-down picture. The buyer's original pricing decision, therefore, is critical and must give proper weight to each of these gross margin factors. This is not a simple exercise. Initial costs, freights, discounts, and transportation are predictable; but costs, markdowns, and inventory shortages are extremely difficult to predict accurately, even though a historical record is available. Nevertheless, markdowns and inventory shortages are highly important factors, and a judgment must be made as to what influence they will have on the final gross margin figure.

Turnover Objectives

It should be quite obvious why turnover objectives affect department store pricing. Certain classifications of merchandise, such as lamps, children's shoes, and men's clothing, require a high investment in inventory which must be priced sufficiently to yield a satisfactory return. Traditionally, these are low-turnover classifications because of the breadth of investment required in relation to sales volume. For example, a certain department may average the same dollar inventory and the same initial markup percentage as another. Yet the first department may produce almost $7.00 of markup for every inventory dollar invested, while the second department produces only $3.00—because of turnover.

Some departments with a high turnover, such as those dealing in drugs, toys, and sporting goods, operate with a traditional low markup. In most cases, discount-type competition forces retail prices down. The use of private brands will often provide a means of maintaining a good stock assortment with a better markup.

Direct and Indirect Expense

Department store accounting generally divides expenses into two categories—direct expense, or that which is directly attributable to a selling department, and the balance, called indirect expense. Since selling departments provide almost all the income in a department store, indirect expense must be prorated against each selling department. In determining his pricing, the buyer should consider that his gross margin must be sufficient to include all categories of expense.

Generally speaking, direct expenses include the following account classifications:

> *Payroll.* That of salespeople, stock help, and cashiers; merchandise managers (pro rata); buyers and assistants; merchandise control and clericals.
>
> *Wrap, pack, and supply expense.*
>
> *Delivery.*
>
> *Other selling.* The cost of other departments, such as mail and phone orders, adjustment, and customer return expense.
>
> *Receiving, checking, and marking.*
>
> *Traveling.*
>
> *Publicity.* Includes gross newspaper advertising less vendors' allowances, advertising preparation, and all other publicity.
>
> *Housekeeping and maintenance.*
>
> *Payroll taxes.*

Indirect expense includes all other items which cannot be charged directly —for example, general management, personnel department and employee benefits, and control and accounting.

Since profitability is the ultimate objective of sound pricing decisions, it is vital that all expenses be considered.

MERCHANDISE CONSIDERATIONS

So far we have discussed cost as well as expense factors related to retail pricing decisions. We have also discussed the effect of turnover. In addition, merchandising factors must be considered before final pricing decisions are made. These factors include competition, merchandise mix, high-risk classifications, profit-opportunity classifications, off-price promotions, the range of services offered to customers, the quality of selling service offered to customers, and the presentation and display of merchandise.

Competition. The importance of competition from all forms of retailing in the trading area of a department store cannot be overlooked. Generally speaking, department stores compete directly on identical items as far as price is concerned. Many stores have comparison shopping offices that regularly shop competitors to be sure that this pricing policy is enforced. Sometimes, however, competition comes from upstairs departments, or from downstairs or budget departments, if it is price-line and not identical-item competition.

Over recent years, certain departments in department stores have become known as discount-type departments because their principal competition for many or most of their classifications is discount stores. In these cases, the competitive pressures force lower original pricing or initial markup. For this reason, it is important to identify and consider the risk-factor and inventory-investment elements. At the same time, overall markup should be improved through creative efforts to sell more profitable merchandise. Furthermore, it is not necessary to carry discount-type classifications in depth, but it is important to have these available to customers if called for. There are certain department stores, however, that prefer to meet discount-type competition head-on and promote these classifications vigorously.

Merchandise mix. Because of the tens of thousands of items that are offered to consumers under one roof, department stores have the problem of providing customer convenience goods regardless of markup. At the same time they have the necessity of producing an overall profit which gives a reasonable return on investment. For this reason, it is important that buyers identify and expand higher-markup classifications. It is also important that display emphasis be placed on better goods with higher markups. Promotional efforts should be spent largely on higher-markup merchandise if better profit results are to be obtained.

Profit-opportunity classifications. Stores have an opportunity to investigate classifications where investment and risk elements are favorable and where potential volume and markup can create larger profits, thus helping the store's mix of business. Many departments have classifications of this type which justify extra attention and creativity.

High-risk classifications. In classifications like misses' better dresses, children's spring coats, and swim suits, and in seasonal shops of all kinds, higher original pricing is needed to cover the unusually high markdown risk. Therefore, pricing must be carefully analyzed by buyers so that risk, expense, and inventory investment are fully considered.

Imports. Fashion-conscious, aggressive department stores today are increasing their sales of imported merchandise for several reasons. A major one is the emphasis being given to creating a good fashion image, whether in the apparel or the home furnishings field, coupled with the pricing flexibility that imports permit. Imports give balance to departments, increase a store's prestige in the community, and broaden the merchandise mix being offered to the consuming public. The inherent risk of high markdown potential in imported merchandise makes it necessary to consider this factor in the original pricing.

Off-price promotions. Off-price promotions are traditional among department stores and other retailing outlets. These include end-of-month clearances, anniversary offerings, and many other familiar devices: August furniture sales; January, May, and August white goods sales; and post-Christmas or post-Easter "specials." There is, however, a growing awareness that off-price promotions should be utilized carefully—particularly in high-investment, high-expense, and discount classifications where day-to-day stocks are most important.

Quality of selling service. Recently, because of the advent of discount stores, a major new emphasis has been developing: the upgrading of selling services among department stores to meet the new retailing competition. This has occurred to such an extent that the discounter himself is being goaded by consumers and competition to provide more selling services and become more competitive with the traditional department store. Although good selling services can increase expense dollars, they also have a significant effect on volume and gross margin improvement which can more than offset this additional dollar cost.

Training salespeople properly in the selling of higher-markup merchandise, discussing the merits of high-profit merchandise with them, educating them to appreciate better-quality goods, and bringing them into the setting of prices or the "retailing" of merchandise have proved good techniques for providing service that will justify better markups.

Presentation and display. The layout of departments to feature high-markup merchandise, along with adequate display facilities, aids materially in the selling of these classifications. This is especially important in areas needing higher markup because of risk, expense, or investment requirements.

Resource Relationships

The finding and developing of the best resources for a particular retail establishment in line with its gross margin objectives, goals, and image are of inestimable importance. Most stores recognize that it is far more profitable and mutually advantageous to concentrate on a limited number of resources rather than play the field. They elect to narrow their choice to those that will best fill their requirements.

Many stores, too, have now developed another tool to determine the value of each of their resources to them. A vendor analysis is produced; this shows volume, initial markup, and markdowns for each resource. By using this tool intelligently, a buyer can determine the net worth of all his resources, comparing one with another. As a result, he can develop the profitable vendors, drop the unprofitable ones, and, if necessary, make replacements.

A key resource will work very closely with a buyer to the mutual advantage of both. Private brands, exclusivity, new items, and special packaging can be obtained. The buyer will then be in a better position to achieve his gross margin objectives.

Private Brands and Exclusivity

In recent years there has been a significant increase in the use of private-brand merchandise sold not only by the huge mail order chains like Penney and Sears but also by the larger department store chains. In many cases, private-brand merchandise in certain classifications has developed a sales volume exceeding that of similar brand-name merchandise. Depending on individual objectives, some retailers choose to use the vehicle of private brands to promote greater profitability in certain classifications and to serve promotional purposes in others. Obviously, private brands give a form of exclusivity which permits greater latitude in pricing.

Another form of exclusivity comes through selling brand-name lines exclusively or semi-exclusively in a given area. This, too, permits greater pricing flexibility.

Manufacturers' Suggested Retails

A suggested retail price by the manufacturer will often allow a good markup. For the most part, consumers consider the manufacturer's suggested retail as a safeguard of their interests, both in prohibiting the retailer to charge a higher price and in giving the consumer a guide to values. In a recent survey, it was found that seven out of every ten consumers consider the manufacturer's suggested retail price a good indication of value and want the practice continued.

Effect of Packaging

Proper packaging will frequently heighten the price image of an item; it almost never harms it. In a recent survey, consumers were shown two identical items—the one packaged, the other not—and were asked to estimate their price. The packaged items were always judged to sell at a higher price than the unpackaged ones.

In the same test, consumers were given a verbal description of the articles prior to being asked how much they sold for. This brief description also improved the items' price image. There is little doubt that even the simplest factual statement about an item affects its price image favorably.

The obvious conclusion is that working with manufacturers to improve packaging and affix description tags can make better markups possible.

Pricing Mechanics

There is no such thing as a "departmental" markup. Establishing a retail price can be a mechanical operation or a challenging decision. Buyers are encouraged to experiment. When the higher markup does not work, management reminds them, they can always revert to the old price.

So far as actual pricing is concerned, several basic concepts are being advanced now:

1. Be bold in the pricing of regular goods.
2. Avoid traditional cost pricing.
3. Retail merchandise on the basis of fashion appeal.
4. Use variable markups on different sizes.
5. Charge extra for special orders.
6. Handle multiple pricing intelligently.

In the final analysis, store pricing over the longer term reflects top management's point of view. It is vitally tied into a store's objectives, whatever they may be. In any one community these can range from building a price-cutting image with a highly promotional flavor to creating a reputation for high-fashion, higher-priced merchandise with limited institutional advertising. The goal can be a broad assortment in soft goods lines or the same breadth in hard goods lines. It can also reflect a hard-hitting basement and budget-price image. There is really no specific limitation on what image a store wishes to project in its area. What *is* limited is the skills necessary to project that image and still meet established profit and return-on-investment objectives.

III. *The Discount House*

Edward W. Cundiff

D ISCOUNT SELLING HAS BEEN A PART OF RETAIL SELLING IN SOME DEGREE FOR as long as there has been retailing. Some entrepreneur has always been willing to shave his price to prevent the loss of a sale or to attract new customers. But the idea of using price as the primary and continuing appeal of a retail establishment is a relatively new one. The idea was originated in food retailing with the development of the low-margin cash-and-carry grocery after World War I, and it reached its refinement in the supermarket. However, the spread of discounting in food retailing was slow; not until the 1950's did these new retailing institutions approach saturation of their market.

EVOLUTION OF DISCOUNT HOUSES

It was inevitable that the idea of discounting would be tried in other merchandise fields. In the 1930's it spread into the retail drug field with the introduction of "cut rate" drug stores. The long-run effect of these price-appeal drug outlets was a reduction in services offered and in general price

PROFESSOR CUNDIFF is Chairman of the Department of Marketing Administration, College of Business Administration, The University of Texas, in Austin.

levels of all drug outlets. It was not until after World War II that discounting was applied to general merchandise lines. This was an area that offered great potential for innovation, since the majority of traditional retailers in these lines, such as department stores, specialty clothing stores, appliance stores, sporting goods stores, dry goods, and furniture stores, were full-service, high-cost operators.

The first discount houses sold mainly appliances. After World War II, when household appliances and other hard goods were hard to get, imaginative retailers who were able to find sources of merchandise set up small retail outlets to sell these goods at discount prices. Since they maintained small inventories, pared services to a minimum, and occupied low-cost retail locations, they were able to underprice traditional competitors. The shortage of merchandise combined with the lower-than-normal prices made consumers willing to go to considerable trouble to shop in such outlets.

The discount house evolved because of inflexibility in the pricing and operating policies of retailers of soft and hard goods. Over a period of years retail margins in lines such as clothing, linen, hardware, and appliances had become fixed through common usage, even though long-term reductions in some operating costs had made these margins unrealistically high in some instances. Recognizing that many such goods could be sold profitably at lower-than-customary margins, a few imaginative entrepreneurs developed discount houses. These first discount houses were small, since their appeal was limited to price alone. Subsequently, however, new merchandising techniques were introduced in discount stores. These new techniques proved attractive to consumers in themselves, but also they often allowed additional reductions in price which further increased their attraction. It was this second wave of innovation that resulted in the development of the modern large discount house.

CHANGE IN PRICING POLICIES

Historically, retailers have taken a myopic view of price. Most are well aware of the contribution that effectively promoted price reductions can make to sales volume. Probably price changes are used as an element in marketing strategy more by retailers than any other businessmen. For example, supermarkets rely heavily on weekend price promotions to attract customers to their premises, and department stores and specialty clothing stores make strong use of seasonal and periodical price promotions to build traffic. However, such price changes are almost invariably of a temporary promotional nature and are followed immediately by a return to "normal" prices.

Although retailers frequently (and some almost constantly) change their prices for short-term promotional purposes, their methods of arriving at base or normal prices are rarely reviewed. Under normal conditions, they price a product by adding a standard percentage of markup to net delivered cost. Thus, if a retailer operates on a normal markup of 33⅓ percent on selling price (or 50 percent on cost), he will price an article that costs him $16.65 at approximately $25.00. He may, of course, modify this price to meet competition—for example, if a competitor is selling the same product at $23.00, he may meet that price (but be reluctant to push it very hard at the lower margin). Or he may adjust the price slightly for psychological reasons, hoping to attract more customers at $24.95 than at $25.00. But, when the net delivered cost of a product changes, the retailer quickly adjusts his price accordingly. Thus, if the cost of the product just described rose to $20.00, the retailer would raise his selling price to $30.00, or $29.95.

Despite their willingness to make temporary price changes for promotional purposes and permanent changes to reflect increasing or decreasing merchandise costs, retailers are very reluctant to adjust prices in line with their own operating costs. The standard markup is treated as something sacred, not subject to change. When retail operating costs rise, with a resulting squeeze on profits, retailers will almost indefinitely resist any change in markup percentage to restore profits. Similarly, when costs go down, retailers very seldom give serious consideration to the possible effects of a reduction in markup on consumer response. It was just such a situation as this in the retail appliance field that led to the development of the earliest discount houses.

During the initial period in the introduction of electrical appliances and radios to the market, the manufacturers relied heavily on the retailers, both to promote these very new products and create a demand for them and to provide servicing for defective or worn products. To compensate the retailers for these important services, the manufacturers suggested retail prices that provided a rather high retail margin—usually 33⅓ percent on the selling price. Gradually, in the next two or three decades, the retailers' investment in these services was reduced. As the manufacturers' brands became well known and were increasingly supported by national advertising, the need for promotion at the retail level almost disappeared. The average retailer became little more than an order taker. At the same time the products he sold were becoming more reliable and were more and more often backed by manufacturer's warranties, drastically reducing the amount of servicing that the retailer needed to provide. The result was that by the late 1940's the traditional 33⅓ percent margin had become unrealistically high. Retail selling costs for appliances had dropped to the point where they could have been sold profitably at a much lower markup.

The manufacturers' pricing policies also contributed to inflexibility, since nearly all manufacturers continued to suggest retail prices based on a 33⅓ percent margin. In fact, a large proportion of the appliance manufacturers had established "fair trade" minimum prices based on a 33⅓ percent margin in the states where this was allowed. A reluctance to disregard manufacturers' list prices or, even more, to break fair-trade laws—when coupled with the natural inertia of retailers toward changes in markup—resulted in an unchanging policy of pricing appliances on the part of traditional dealers despite the long-term reduction in costs.

A few enterprising individuals, however, recognized the potential for large profits from the sale of appliances at lower-than-normal margins. They were not bound by custom in figuring their margins, and they were willing to risk the displeasure of appliance manufacturers in undercutting their suggested list prices. Even the threat of legal sanctions in those situations where fair-trade laws existed was not enough to counteract the attraction of a rich potential profit.

By the early 1950's a number of small hole-in-the-wall discounters had developed in major cities. Their sole appeal was price. Little or no promotion was attempted beyond that of bringing the name of the store to the attention of consumers, and much of this was achieved by word of mouth. Physical facilities and fixtures were kept to a minimum, and locations were based on site availability rather than consumer convenience. Services were almost eliminated; cash-and-carry was the rule. These new stores, with prices averaging between 20 and 30 percent below manufacturers' list, quickly attracted an ever widening circle of customers.

CHANGE IN MERCHANDISING TECHNIQUES

The growth potential for the small-appliance discount house was limited; but, when its price-oriented operating philosophy was applied to the entire broad area of general merchandise, the potential for growth became very large. By the middle of the 1950's a number of retailers were applying the discounting method to the entire gamut of products classified under the heading of general merchandise, including clothing (men's, women's, and children's), hardware, sporting goods, furniture, jewelry, drugs, and often even food.

These large discount houses have sometimes been described as soft-goods supermarkets, and the description is an apt one since it recognizes a strong similarity in merchandising techniques. Both types of retailers sell at lower prices than their competitors, and these low prices are made possible by similar operating policies. Perhaps the most important of these policies is an emphasis on high sales volume and merchandise turnover coupled with a low gross margin. By concentrating on a rapid turnover of merchandise, these retailers are able to keep their inventory investment low and thus reduce the return of income necessary to support this investment. In addition, management is willing to settle for a lower gross margin per dollar of sales because the great increase in total sales volume produces an increase in total dollar margin.

A second important operating policy common to supermarkets and discount houses is the reduction of services. Essentially both are cash-and-carry operations. The discount house normally delivers only those items, such as heavy appliances and furniture, that the customer cannot carry away himself; the supermarket normally delivers nothing. Yet the competitors of these two types of retailers often provide full delivery service. Department stores, specialty clothing stores, and furniture stores typically provide delivery service at the customer's request; so does the full-service food store, which in fact uses delivery service as one of its strongest appeals. Again, both discount houses and supermarkets sell normally on a cash basis, with the customer paying for the goods at the time of purchase. The one exception is that discount houses may offer conditional sales contracts with repayment on an installment basis in the case of expensive items such as refrigerators. Yet open-account credit is one of the major competitive appeals of department stores, service food stores, and other competitors of these retailers.

A third major service that is greatly reduced in the discount house, as in the supermarket, is the help of sales people. Operations are organized primarily on a self-service basis with merchandise displayed in a way that allows the customer to help himself. A few store employees are available to answer questions and locate desired merchandise when necessary, but they tend to spend the majority of their time in stock-keeping activities.

Like the supermarket, the discount house is usually located in a residential or suburban area near the consumer. The small early houses often occupied low-rent locations in central city areas, and customers were expected to seek them out, but the modern stores are near large concentrations of potential customers. Discount houses must be located farther apart than supermarkets because each requires a much larger pool of potential buyers; one expert estimates that each major discount house must have a minimum population of 50,000 in the market it serves.

It would seem likely that discount houses would benefit from being in major shopping centers, but there has been little opportunity to prove this until very recently. In the past, shopping-center managements have refused space to discounters because of the violent opposition of such other tenants as department stores and clothing stores, who feared the competition. There was also a widespread feeling that a discount house would lower the quality image of a shopping center. Because of this opposition, discounters have found it necessary to locate their stores in separate buildings, but they have often found sites close to shopping centers where they have been able to benefit from the center's promotional efforts in attracting shoppers to the area. And recently, as discounters have begun to achieve the legitimacy that time eventually confers on all new retailing institutions, and as shopping-center operators have come to realize that not all discount houses carry low-quality merchandise, discounters have begun to find it possible to locate in shopping centers.

Whether a discount house is inside a shopping center or not, it needs the same general kind of location. It should have close access to a large population; it should be located on a major traffic artery with easy access; and it should provide abundant free parking.

PRESENT POSITION OF THE DISCOUNT HOUSE

The growth of the discount house has been a very rapid one in the American market. In a period of 20 years, it has come to occupy an important position in the retail structure. In 1966 there were nearly 2,700 discount houses currently in operation, with a combined floor space of 172 million square feet.[1] The combined sales of these stores were in excess of $12 billion, or ap-

---

[1] *Discount Store News*, August 22, 1966, p. 17.

proximately 24 percent of all sales of general-merchandise-type stores.[2] The average store has about 64,000 square feet of floor space and achieves annual sales of approximately $4.3 million, and the rate of growth is continuing—with a trend toward larger stores. The 268 new discount stores that were opened in 1965 had an average of 75,000 square feet of floor space.

It is too early to predict the ultimate role of discount houses in the American retail structure. In the past, each new retailing institution has gone through a period of growth and expansion before leveling off at some more or less stable share of the market. Discount houses are still growing, and the rate of growth has been much faster than for most other major retail institutions. The ultimate market share for discounters is anybody's guess.

The more optimistic forecasters, who like to compare discount houses to supermarkets, point out that supermarkets have expanded until they account for approximately 90 percent of food sales. They believe the discount house can achieve as large a share of the general-merchandise market as the supermarket has of the food market. The more conservative forecasters point out that consumer buying patterns are not the same for general merchandise and food. They believe that a much larger proportion of consumers will prefer and demand a full range of services in buying general merchandise than in buying food. Naturally, the managers of the traditional full-service general-merchandise stores are among the strongest proponents of this view, and their discounting competitors accuse them of indulging, at least to some degree, in wishful thinking. Many full-service food retailers were guilty of this kind of inability to face reality and adjust to change and, eventually, were forced out of business.

There is very likely an important element of truth in the argument that consumers will continue to prefer more service in the purchase of general merchandise, but no one knows how many consumers prefer how much service when the alternative of reduced service brings with it liberal price reductions. Consumer preferences for service may also vary widely among different lines of general merchandise; for example, more consumers may want the help of sales clerks on clothing than on hardware or toys. Thus the extent of the discount house's penetration of the market may vary considerably among categories of merchandise.

At this time the growth trend of discount-store sales has shown no sign

---

[2] *Ibid.*

of leveling off; so the final percentage of market penetration is still unpredictable. Conservative guesses place it somewhere below 50 percent of the market; liberal guesses place it higher.

EFFECT OF DISCOUNTERS ON PRICING

Discount houses have markedly increased the importance of price as a factor in the selection of retail outlets for general merchandise. An increasing number of consumers turn to discount stores to obtain their needs at lower prices, forgoing the more luxurious surroundings, the help of sales clerks, and the many additional services of such retailers as department stores and clothing stores.

As the traditional retailers have observed the increasing impact of discounters, they have adjusted some of their own policies with respect to price. Always aware of the value of price as a short-term promotional appeal, they have turned their attention, also, to the use of lower base prices as a means of attracting customers. In the home-appliance line, where discount competition has been strongest and of longest duration, traditional retailers have lowered margins. Formerly, appliances were often allocated an unduly heavy share of overhead expense; now, more realistic cost allocations have made it possible to sell these items profitably at lower prices. In other lines, such as hard goods, it has been possible to reduce costs (and hence prices) by the installation of self-service or semi-self-service. Traditional retailers in the general-merchandise lines have taken a more careful look at customary markups and reduced costs, where possible, to allow the reduction of prices.

Discounters have in fact been responsible in some degree for a general reevaluation and reduction of prices on the part of many of their competitors. Even so, although the price spread between these competitors has been reduced, discount house prices are still lower, and the amount of difference varies depending on the kind of merchandise.

Discount houses may also have had some effect on retail food pricing in certain instances. It was pointed out earlier that the operating methods of supermarkets and discount houses are very similar. Under these circumstances it was natural for the two types of retailers to combine forces under one roof. A fairly sizable number of discount houses have incorporated food items as part of their merchandise lines. When these food sections are operated as leased departments, their prices are not likely to vary in total from those of their supermarket competitors, since they are seldom able to achieve greater operating efficiency than the supermarkets have already achieved.

There has been some evidence to support the fact that these food departments, when operated by the discount-house management, are operated as price leaders to build store traffic.[3] The effect of such a pricing policy is to squeeze even tighter the margins of competing supermarkets. And, even when discount-house food departments are not used as price leaders or loss leaders, they follow a pricing policy slightly different from their supermarket competitors. They rely more heavily on lower-than-normal margins because they make less use of weekly price promotions.

✦   ✦   ✦

The discount house is here to stay as an important part of the retail structure. It developed to fill a need; many consumers were more concerned with the prices of general merchandise than traditional retailers thought they were. It is still too early to predict the ultimate impact of the discounters in terms of market share, but these new retail institutions have already had a noticeable effect on the pricing of a wide variety of merchandise.

---

[3] A recent study in Austin, Texas, supported this view; it was found that the discount food department undersold neighboring supermarkets. See Cundiff, E. W., and R. C. Andersen, "Competitive Food Pricing," *Journal of Retailing,* Spring 1963.

Pricing by Product Type

I. Consumer Products

Sherman P. Haight, Jr.

P RICING IS OBVIOUSLY A CRITICAL FACTOR IN THE SALE OF CONSUMER PRODUCTS. From the producer's point of view it is inseparable from considerations of cost and profit—of marketing channels, sales promotion, and product attributes. In his mind, too, it is associated with such demand factors as competitive situation, economic climate, and a host of other variables. For example, freedom of pricing may be limited by established retail price lines or margins—or by one's own practice of leading or following. Or custom, habit, inertia, and even mystique may govern the establishment of a price.

Experience generally indicates that pricing has been yielding, though slowly and stubbornly, to the mathematics of science. This is so partly because cumbersome calculations now are being handled swiftly and easily by the computer. But the great number of variables involved in pricing are not readily quantified; their translation into machine language entails many difficulties. Artful judgment, therefore, is still of the utmost importance in pricing, which must eventually be termed an inexact science.

Variables aside, pricing is properly governed by objective. One might ask, to be sure, *"Does* good pricing maximize sales or profits?" Again, ex-

SHERMAN P. HAIGHT, JR. is President, E-Z Mills, Inc., New York City.

perience indicates that pricing, by itself, does not achieve this common objective. Hence the necessity for understanding the complex cause-and-effect interaction of the other elements which contribute to sales and profits under the various conditions which may exist for a given product in its particular market. Hence, also, the need for carefully weighed judgment and for keeping in sight, throughout the pricing process, the simple principle of "supply and demand."

PROFIT—AND PRICING—CRITERIA

Any one or a combination of objectives may be involved to a varying degree in any pricing decision. Growth on either a short- or a long-term basis, share of market, and defense against entry all are familiar objectives of the forward-thinking marketer. Another is market segmentation, which calls for pricing specific products so as to develop sales in certain territories or pricing to meet regional competitive situations that are not representative of national preference.

The profit objective and the share which each product must contribute to it often are matters of company policy, carefully delineated in the marketing plan. Where this is the case, profit is a dominant pricing objective. Nevertheless, such a policy cannot be applied with mechanical rigidity because profit is a function of many activities. The effect of a stated price level—for example, its influence on volume and the absorption of burden—requires precise calculation before the real profit which can be expected to result from it can be determined.

This type of consideration supports pricing's role as the paymaster, and it makes forward planning a definite necessity. At the point when a new product is being introduced, for instance, it will certainly be desirable (and it may be possible) to forecast the strength of subsequent competition which may require a price reduction. The price of this new product, therefore, must cover all costs of profitable distribution—including the cost of a subsequent price reduction. If the original price has not left room for such action, a market may well have been developed without a reasonable chance of lasting profit.

Sometimes pricing is affected by the need to increase the size of individual orders for the purpose of generating economies of manufacturing or handling. Then, too, it may be used to attract new channels of distribution. For example, selling through wholesalers is now receiving considerable retail attention as a means of distribution owing to the current need to increase volume on the same or lower investment; therefore, a new look is being taken at pricing for wholesalers.

Pricing for leadership as an objective may aim at supporting either a line of products or an individual product which stands alone. It is almost always a consideration at the time when the merchandise is being introduced; it seldom enters into repricing strategy during the life of the product or products.

INITIAL PRICING AND REPRICING

To be sure that one has properly identified and codified the appropriate criteria before entering into a pricing decision can save great disappointment at a later date.

Though, as we have seen, there is no price which can maximize sales or profits, long- or short-term, there is an optimum or best possible price which will suit the various product and promotional factors contributing to the sales and profit objective. A relationship exists between the cost and the price, not only of the product itself, but also of such associated elements as promotion and standard margins for the chosen distributors. In considering original pricing as the paymaster, one must decide whether there is room to cover the cost of the ideal product or whether that cost can stand paring, without undue damage to the product, to meet an inflexible price line. This is indeed a sensitive area, for, if costs are inadequately covered, opportunities may be strangled. If, say, there is not enough provision for promotion of an innovation which requires consumer education, the product will have little opportunity to find its way into the market. And, by the same token, if the margins provided by pricing are not attractive to retailers or wholesalers, they may buy the product but attempt to hedge against possible loss by under-the-counter selling or promotional soft-pedaling.

Repricing, which is ideally foreseen at the time of original pricing, should be regulated by codified policies to the furthest possible extent. If a product is priced at a premium—that is, above the market—its repricing should follow the same policy even though the market, in general, may have shifted to a new level.

It is often planned that a product be a leader or a follower. Repricing a follower is done almost by rote. But, if the product is a leader in its field, then repricing it to meet a changed level of competition or market strength may require careful assessment and ingenuity of a high order.

Codified policies may be difficult, if not impossible, to follow when repricing becomes necessary. However, forward planning at the initial stage of product introduction can provide adequate allowance for what could otherwise be an unwarranted loss. Scheduling repricing for a product as it moves from the introductory stage to maturity is one example. By the same token, repricing to meet a competitive move can be part of a codified policy that is laid down in advance.

In initial pricing, the policy is often one of "When in doubt, start high and work down." This usually results in repricing at a lower level after the product's first experience on the market. A change in economic conditions, action by a competitor, the effect of a substitute product introduced at a lower price, a change in raw material costs—all may suggest the wisdom of repricing.

Too often there is a reluctance to change price regardless of the arguments for so doing. This reluctance may stem from a policy of following rather than leading or from the feeling that lower prices will not alter demand substantially. In the opposite case, management may fear that increasing prices—despite apparent cost justification—will substantially lower demand. But reluctance to move in either direction, unhappily, can be the result of sheer inertia.

THE CONSUMER MARKET

There are discernible differences between the pricing of consumer products and industrial products. Industrial purchasers, for example, tend to be more knowledgeable and more rational than the general consumer. They deal more directly; in negotiating price, they take a broad spectrum of variables into account. The consumer, on the other hand, generally is less knowledgeable and more emotional.

The emotional requirements of a product—be they esthetic specifications or status needs—are powerful impellents. Joel Dean [1] speaks of the "illusionary differentiation" as being more difficult with producers' goods than with consumer goods. It is true that the industrial purchasing agent's motivation may differ from the consumer's by degree alone, the purchasing agent's order of supplies for a small office approaching the consumer's pur-

---

[1] Dean, Joel, *Managerial Economics*, Prentice-Hall, Inc., 1951, Chapters 7–9.

chase of paper and pencils for home use. But, if esthetics mattered not at all to the industrial purchasing agent, lathes and cranes—which hardly fit the consumer's shopping list—would look far uglier; and, if status symbols were meaningless in industry, many computer installations would be either less elaborate or nonexistent. On the other hand, the consumer may approach the purchase of his one automobile as scientifically as the purchasing expert who must buy cars or trucks by the fleet.

In establishing the prices of consumer goods, one must appreciate these and other attributes of the consumer market. It is further characterized, for example, by *choice*. First of all, the consumer has available to him substitute products which he can and does measure one against another in the same or competitive product lines. Second, he can choose between spending for products and spending for nonmaterial items such as services. The consumer's choice may, in fact, be the decision to save, not to spend on either product or service.

Even so, the market is constantly increasing for most consumer products—expansion is manifest in its numerical size, in its total wealth, and in the dispersion of income. To a large extent this big market is no longer price-dominated. There are more purchasers with a wider range of gratifiable desires. People who want many kinds of satisfaction are willing and able to pay for them, and the features added to the products they buy for this purpose must be significant and somehow observable. Thus price becomes a selection factor to be judged in combination with other purchasing impellents.

The make-up of the growing market for consumer goods permits some freedom of pricing to provide for product features which will gratify consumer desires, for the necessary promotion, and for other such considerations. However, there are still segments of the market in which price remains dominant. In these segments the nonprice factors in pricing may have to give way.

THE IMPELLENCE QUOTIENT

Wingate and Friedlander [2] suggest a method of weighing price and the other selection factors through the construction of an "impellence quotient." The numerator of the impellence quotient contains all the factors except

---

[2] Wingate, John W., and Joseph S. Friedlander, *The Management of Retail Buying*, Prentice-Hall, Inc., 1963, Chapter 14.

price—superior quality, degree of advertising, point-of-sale display, everything that influences customers' decisions. The denominator of the quotient is the price charged for the product.

The value of the impellence quotient lies in its interpretation by the marketer. The higher the value, the theory goes, the more the prospect will be impelled to buy.

There are, of course, ways in which the value of the quotient can be raised. Repricing (which generally means lowering the price) is the easiest, but it is also the most readily emulated by competition. Strengthening the nonprice elements in the numerator requires a greater combination of inherent talent and acquired skills; it is therefore more difficult for competitors to emulate.

Quantifying the complex elements in the numerator is, in fact, loaded with pitfalls. Pricing research is a tool of the marketer which has had considerable use in this connection; and, for entry into a known field or for repricing, the statistical analysis of peak-volume price lines has been an effective guide, although the availability of information is sometimes a problem. By the same token, considerable work has been done in the field of consumer surveys to test attitudes and intentions. The results, however, have been of great interest to the marketer but have generally not proved acceptable as a guide to pricing.

The problem is to arrive at a true rather than a distorted picture of the factors in any pricing decision—and there are many hazards. Yet, prone though it is to subjectively influenced conjecture, the construction of the impellence quotient does provide a means of positioning the elements of selection in such a manner as to apply some cause-and-effect reasoning to that decision.

THE DEMAND MULTIPLIER

Naturally the traditional methods of pricing are used in connection with consumer goods. One of these is "cost plus," whereby the costs of direct labor and materials plus promotion and general overhead are combined and a predetermined margin of profit is added to arrive at the selling price. Elaborations of this procedure vary almost with the number of firms in business. Its virtue lies in the fact that it is convenient and quick, providing the shortest time response to changing conditions.

In its simpler forms, cost-plus pricing does not require a sophisticated system or facilities. Its greatest fault is its failure to account for the demand multiplier which governs total revenue with its attendant effect on both costs and profits. To be more specific, the costs used in the cost-plus method are based on typical or average experience, while the actual costs may vary with the success of the current pricing decisions—a feedback effect which is taken into account when other, more sophisticated methods of calculating costs are used.

For instance, so-called "demand centered" pricing is geared to the exploitation of the estimated demand for a product. As an example, the accepted price for a certain item may be approximately four dollars. When an innovation in this category is under consideration, the pricing formula is worked backward to see whether the new or improved product can be made to sell at four dollars. The selling price must allow enough margin to make the product attractive to its channels of distribution and enough sales promotion to exploit a substantial portion of the estimated demand. It must also provide enough profit to warrant adding the product to the line. If the product cannot be justified on this basis, then it must have other, overriding virtues.

Before reaching a decision it is often useful to determine whether there may not be a market for an upgraded version of the product that would sell at five dollars, for example. If such a market exists, what kind of significant and observable features can be added to the four-dollar product to make its impellence quotient more attractive at the higher price? This may be a very strong consideration, for it is conceivable that a small amount of additional labor and materials will be more than offset by the new retail price. In other words, the upgraded product may result in a higher unit profit and enough volume to assure increased gross-margin dollars as well. Manufacturers whose profits on particular items have been squeezed by competitive pressure over the years may in this way find new and profitable markets awaiting exploitation.

The converse of this situation may also exist; that is, the product may need a lower price than four dollars to uncover sufficient demand. Working backward from the conjectured ideal retail price, where can we find the necessary savings? Only product knowledge and ingenuity can answer this question, but a lower margin per item may, at an increased level of sales, increase the company's total gross margin as compared with that resulting from the original, high price.

MATHEMATICAL MODEL BUILDING

In the foregoing examples we have combined the different pricing variables, determining by unit price the optimum revenues to be generated and multiplying by estimated sales response. The result is still burdened by conjecture, for there is no law relating sales potential to each possible price. Product potential measured in terms of price-demand elasticity under any given set of conditions still requires an estimate of competitive reaction as well as consumer response.

There is in progress a serious effort on the part of many experts to account for these variables in pricing decisions. Mathematicians, for example, are able to build models of the workings of these variables as integrated in pricing decisions of record. By making changes in the models, it is possible to simulate results under a whole series of alternative decisions. The necessary calculations are of course facilitated by the computer.

Even though the use of a mathematical model in dealing with pricing variables still requires conjecture, it is conjecture on a more orderly, better-structured, and more reliable level. True, actual work in this area has not yet had much practical application, but it does seem to hold promise. It may in time afford management the opportunity to choose the combination of variables which will best achieve the required objective in pricing.

CONSTRAINTS ON PRICING

Another facet of the pricing problem, so far as consumer products are concerned, is the constraints which very definitely exist. These stem from a variety of limiting conditions. A high price, for example, may be supported by patents, a unique means of manufacture which is not readily available to a competitor, control over raw materials through an integrated operation, uniqueness of product, or specialization of the labor force. These elements tend toward a constricted market situation which lessens the supply of a given product and, therefore, competition for it.

But a high price level may stem from a multitude of other reasons as well. High research and development costs, for example, will inevitably influence unit price. So will limited production, a limited market, or extraordinary promotional expense, as for an educational campaign planned to introduce a new type of product. An item, as noted, may be priced at the top of its bracket because attractive margins must be provided for distributors.

A short demand cycle, other inventory-markdown risks, the need for quick recapture of a large initial investment—these too may create higher-than-normal prices.

On the other hand, the objective of getting a big jump on competition or the desire to discourage competitive products from entering the field at all may influence a manufacturer to set a lower-than-normal price level. One example is the planned intention to earn low unit margins but produce large gross-margin-dollar returns by gaining substantial sales volume. Others are the decision to use leaders in a product line mix and the assumption of high demand elasticity in the market.

What further constraints are there on the pricing of consumer items? The accepted pricing structure among retailers certainly is a limiting factor, particularly with apparel and other basic products for which the establishment of specific price points is a strongly held merchandising practice. Moreover, the pricing of an individual item is sometimes influenced by the pricing of the product line to which the item belongs. It is therefore necessary to consider the effect on the total line when studying the cost and profit elements of pricing. In justifying a low-profit item, it is important, above all, to avoid an artificially lowered incremental cost or share of overhead.

And, finally, there are price differentials—as much a part of pricing as the stated list prices which appear in the catalogue. These differentials may represent trade discounts, usually founded on accepted practice, for a particular product sold through a particular class of distributor. Or they may reflect quantity discounts, cash discounts, geographical differentials, freight allowances, and advertising and promotion allowances, to name the most generally used types. Sometimes they are established to lure new customers or enter new markets; sometimes they provide a means of meeting special competitive conditions, encouraging prompt payment, or selling a product which requires special presentation at the point of sale.

Whatever these limiting factors may be, they must be taken into account in the pricing process along with the variables. For—to repeat—pricing is not an exact science; judgment remains the essential ingredient in every sound decision.

II. *Industrial Products*

Leigh Carter

THE PRICING OF INDUSTRIAL PRODUCTS REQUIRES EXTENSIVE RESEARCH AND A thorough knowledge of the specific markets under consideration. In order to clarify the many problems faced by management in this area, it may be helpful first to examine the broad types of supplier-buyer relationships that exist in industrial selling and the special situations to which they lend themselves.

In general, supplier-buyer relationships in the industrial field may be grouped under three headings:

1. *The specialty-product relationship.* This presupposes a specialty product line, usually backed up by substantial service benefits, which requires a high level of creative selling. In such a relationship, the seller literally creates the purchase by developing the need in the buyer's mind. As a result, the buyer tends to blind himself to the intrinsic value of the product and, instead, focus on all the associated benefits.

2. *The inquiry/bid relationship.* The system of requesting bids is

LEIGH CARTER is Executive Vice President, The Tremco Manufacturing Company, Cleveland, Ohio.

most commonly used where the buyer is sophisticated in the technical requirements of his product and is also competent to test and evaluate the supplier's compliance or lack of compliance with the specifications, which, in considerable detail, set forth those needs. The system requires a fair amount of technical expertise on the part of both buyer and seller; as a result, the buyer screens out the product costs related to service and fringe benefits and obtains prices based on basic product costs.

3. *The contractual relationship.* Just as the specialty-product relationship allows considerable opportunity to establish prices on the basis of extensive services and the inquiry/bid relationship screens much of this out, the contractual relationship tends to be based solely on economic analysis. It usually exists where the transaction involves a large annual purchase including many basic materials: coal, oil, steel, and the like.

Obviously there is a certain overlapping of these three general types of buyer-supplier relationships. They do, however, serve to establish extremes and point out the very real differences which may exist within the industrial product market and their overall effect on pricing practice.

CONSIDERATIONS IN PRICING INDUSTRIAL PRODUCTS

Historically, product pricing has been the province of financial management with the advice of marketing management. But under the marketing concept, with the company's marketing management playing its proper role, pricing too assumes major importance.

In the cycle of need, identification, research, product development, product promotion, and sale, pricing is really the key factor—a barometer indicating success or failure. If, in the final analysis, after all the costly steps involved in bringing a product to market have been taken, a price cannot be successfully established which results in a satisfactory margin-volume relationship, then the entire process has been a failure.

Looked upon in this way, pricing is an integral part of the entire marketing process and, as such, must lie in the province of appropriate executives with normal authority to make or approve decisions.

Basic objective. If there were only one prime, constant objective in product pricing, then administration might be relatively simple. However, there may be a variety of objectives dependent upon the particular situation. These may include:

1. Pricing which will be so competitive that a very large volume and share of the market will be achieved.
2. Pricing to allow marketing of a product which is necessary to complete the line but which represents an area where low-cost competitors have an advantage.
3. Pricing to provide maximum return and so cover extensive research and manufacturing investments.
4. Pricing to drive out lower-cost competitors who otherwise could operate successfully under an "umbrella" price set by the leader.
5. Pricing to provide the means of distribution deemed desirable.

The objective in a particular pricing decision may in fact cover the entire range of marketing objectives which exist in the development, sale, and perpetuation of a product line. To generalize, however, there is just one central objective which will guide marketing policy in any normal situation: to achieve the maximum return consistent with the "real" advantages provided the customer and consistent with maintenance of product leadership without competitive jeopardy.

Timing. Proper timing of the pricing decision is fundamental to success. It is revealed clearly in the fundamental marketing principle that *true success comes not from developing a market for a product but from developing a product for a market.* Because pricing is, as we have said, a barometer of success in marketing an industrial product, it must come very early in the product-development process. There is little purpose in investing all the development funds in an "equation" which from the beginning does not prove out.

Procedure. The ideal sequence in the typical industrial product-development project is as follows:

1. Identification of market need.
2. Generalized concept of product.
3. Marketing statement starting with optimum market price and working backward through sales cost, promotion cost, support costs, and special capital expenditures to arrive at the maximum allowable manufactured cost.

4. Feasibility study by research and manufacturing.
5. Establishment of a final plan.

Experience indicates that while this procedure probably is followed in most industrial firms, it is nevertheless difficult to retain complete objectivity during the pricing process. Most of the information must be based on estimates, not facts, and those departments of the company that share enthusiasm for the project may be optimistic in their estimates. Unusual management skill must be applied to testing the merit of the equation.

CONTRASTING APPROACHES TO THE PRICING DECISION

Managing the pricing decision in a highly competitive marketplace thus has become a complicated task. It may be an overgeneralization to say that there are two basic approaches, but this broad classification will at least provide a framework for this brief discussion of product-pricing theory as it concerns industrial products.

One approach stems from an orientation that is largely internal. It presumes a variety of fixed factors which eliminate any significant creativity in product pricing. Within this concept, the pricing decision is largely predetermined by the application of existing formulas relating to the cost system used by the firm. In most cases, the system will not tolerate the establishment of such variables as volume ranges and support costs. This general approach usually has the desirable aspect of insuring profitability on any significant volume of product sold, but it is so conservative that it may hamstring planned innovation.

The second general approach to industrial pricing should probably be described as market-oriented. It does not presume that the pricing decision must be controlled solely by historic internal cost factors; it merely uses such data as a basis for strategic market planning. Within this concept, a whole series of variables can be introduced in an attempt to arrive at optimum pricing. This approach utilizes the "marginal income" principle and allows sales management to set up varying objectives as to volume, color or container mix, distribution method, and so on for testing purposes.

The effect of these two approaches to pricing is perhaps best illustrated by actual experience. For example, a large manufacturer of fiber glass some years ago decided to expand into the pleasure-craft marine field. This company had traditionally been a basic supplier to large industries; also, it was accustomed to a type of marketing which resulted in long-term contractual relationships. In developing its prices for the new market, management used all its historical experience and, from a largely internal orientation, developed what it considered to be optimum pricing.

While, however, the company was successful in marketing to the marine field, it discovered after several years that profits were less than anticipated. One factor alone describes the character of the problem: The marine market turned out to be made up of small undercapitalized firms, with the result that the average order size was quite small. Moreover, and for the same reason, credit extension was a considerable risk factor. The company ended by expanding its credit department from two or three employees to a staff of twelve. And the established prices were such that management found itself constantly trying to increase order size and very reluctant to take the average credit risk.

In retrospect, it was clear that proper analysis at the time of original pricing might well have revealed that considerably higher prices would have been tolerated provided the company was prepared to process relatively small orders and extend liberal credit. With these more realistic prices and resulting profit margins, management might have decided to support the market in this way instead of withdrawing in an effort to minimize the firm's losses.

In contrast, a company which took the trouble to analyze a very competitive price situation in a market where products had traditionally been sold directly to the user found a different way to effect optimum pricing. Acknowledging that it did not have product advantages which would allow it to be other than completely competitive, it established an equation which provided for a new channel of distribution and the establishment of local warehousing. By being the only supplier that recognized the importance of local stocks to the user who preferred to purchase in small quantities and not tie up his capital in large stocks, the company was able to charge a premium price that more than offset the cost of the warehouse operation.

The lesson to be learned from these and other examples is that skillful management can establish a whole set of market variables prior to the pricing decision which may permit the development of a unique marketing position and thereby achieve optimum pricing. Such aggressive action to a large extent allows the firm to control its own product destiny. To the contrary, recognition of competitors' weakness at a later date, once pricing has become well established in the marketplace, may not allow other than defensive moves which, often, fail to accomplish pricing objectives.

A Guide to Evaluation

The pricing process is a guide to evaluating product or system superiority. In the development of new products or systems, there are certain points which tend to force objective analysis.

The first such point probably comes at the completion of the initial feasibility study. At this point, when modest assets have been invested, a report of probable success and cost is presented to management. This usually is the time when the company must decide whether or not to commit major assets and so allow development to proceed. Faced with the investment of considerable resources, management is likely to be quite objective, measuring the probability of success in terms of cost, return, and so on.

At the other end of the product-development process there is another unusual opportunity for management to evaluate objectively what has been achieved—during the pricing decision. It is at this point that sales management must indicate unmistakably on a hard, cold basis the worth of the entire project. Obviously, if all the evaluations tend toward favorable pricing, at least in a preliminary way, the project has been a success. If, however, pricing is not favorable, this is a clear indication that something is wrong: Research has not achieved all its objectives, new competition has come into the market during the life of the project, the application requirements have changed, or whatever the problem may be. So, while pricing which will not bring a proper return is certainly cause for review to isolate areas of weakness in the product-development process, it also reveals a constructive course of action.

What we are saying is that an inadequate price relative to investment means that the product's value in the marketplace is almost surely inadequate. Recognition of this fact should direct management's energies toward re-evaluating the product or system to build in more value. This may be accomplished through actual changes in the product, through the addition of marketing advantages, through changes in market direction, and so forth. The important thing to remember is that the pricing decision has provided a warning signal indicating the need for restudy; in other words, an opportunity to hold up introduction of the product until plans can be revised and implemented on a more profitable basis.

Maintenance of Product Pricing in the Market

One of industry's most difficult problems is the maintenance of favorable pricing in the marketplace.

Typically, the successful marketing of an unusual product is conducive to the rapid introduction of competitive products at lower prices. There is probably no absolute defense against this sort of competitive action, but the maintenance of favorable pricing may be influenced by specific steps during the exclusive sales period.

Contact with company purchasing departments. Provided the product is not sold on the basis of a long-term contract but is one that requires constant contact, its position with company purchasing departments must be established during the period when the seller enjoys a monopoly on it. To the extent that these purchasing departments attempt to "screen out" nonessential benefits and get down to basics, the seller must make sure that the product's real value is not lost by oversight or lack of understanding. This is a constant selling job that must continue indefinitely.

Competitive intelligence. It is becoming increasingly clear to the industrial community that action based on internal factors does not always have a favorable effect on the market and that the focus of action must be based on external factors as well. Competitive intelligence, properly fed into the marketing plan, can often result in innovations which preempt the competitor and allow favorable pricing to be maintained, whereas lack of competitive intelligence may result in a defensive position. And the usual defensive action, unfortunately, is erosion of existing pricing.

Continuation of research efforts. At times, industrial management falls into the trap of redirecting all research when a new product has obviously succeeded in the marketplace—on the logic that the "job has been done" and research is required for other product lines. This decision can lead to disaster. Competitors come into the marketplace benefiting from identification of the leader's weak features. Should the followers overcome these weak features, the leader is left in jeopardy, particularly if research has been turned off.

From another point of view, research has reached its peak of competence at the time when a product is introduced to the market. It is therefore logical that the continuation of development work to a limited degree may result in significant innovations during the exclusive sale period which will be the most effective means of combating competition and maintaining premium pricing. Serious consideration should obviously be given to continuing major research work on developed products as a prime basis for maintaining long-term profitability.

To sum up: In organizations where product pricing is an integral part of the whole marketing process from the establishment of research objectives to the maintenance of the market, where pricing is practiced within the marketing concept and is responsive to external market considerations as opposed to internal factors alone, it should play a dynamic role in achieving preeminence in the company's chosen field.

III. *Industrial Property Rights Under License*

R. Granger Benson

IT IS GENERALLY CONCEDED THAT, EVERYTHING ELSE BEING EQUAL, THE DIRECT manufacture or assembly of products in a chosen market by a parent company or its subsidiary, or by a company in which the parent has a proprietary interest, is preferable to indirect manufacture through the medium of licensing industrial property rights. Many sorts of licensing arrangements are, of course, entered into for various purposes under varying circumstances; the term "industrial property rights" is used here to mean all types of rights under patents, trademarks, designs, copyrights, know-how, technical data, and certain categories of technical aid and assistance. Direct manufacture is, however, generally the more permanent approach to a promising market and should provide the best opportunity for deriving the most benefits from potential growth and expansion.

In addition, direct participation in the economy of a market, with complete control over one's own operations, will normally result in a greater financial return over the long term. Under these circumstances, the possibil-

R. GRANGER BENSON is President, Foreign Operations Service, Inc., with headquarters in Essex, Connecticut.

ity of a direct investment in plant and equipment, training of supervisory personnel, and attendant capital expenditures should be carefully considered before deciding definitely on indirect manufacture through license, with less or no direct control over licensee operations, as the desirable alternative.

However, if conditions in the market are not favorable for direct investment, if capital is not available, if the product or products do not warrant the investment involved, or if the risk is considered too great, it may be preferable to license a suitable established manufacturer in the market under consideration. A licensing arrangement can provide a regular source of income with a minimum of investment. Furthermore, in the event local manufacture by the licensor is contemplated at a later date, a licensing arrangement in the interim period will provide a test of the developing potential in the market, thus enabling management to make a decision as to the practicability of direct local manufacture upon the termination of the licensing contract.

One of the principal disadvantages of licensing as compared to direct manufacture is that the licensor exercises no direct control over the management or operations of the licensee. He may be contributing to the growth of a possible competitor—even putting that competitor "in business." Should the licensor at some future date—as, for example, upon the termination of the license contract—decide that time and circumstances now justify direct manufacture, he may be faced with an unexpectedly strong rival in the shape of his former licensee, to whom he, as licensor, has given the tools (that is, the technical know-how) to compete successfully.

To forestall just such an eventuality, an increasing number of U.S. licensors are giving serious consideration to licensing arrangements which permit stock participation in the licensee company and representation on its board of directors, as well as royalty and other payments. In such cases, the royalty rates are generally lower than in the straight royalty type of agreement. Such an arrangement with stock participation provides for a measure of licensor control over licensee management and operations and lends a degree of permanency to the relationship between the two parties.

In short, despite the advantages offered by direct investment and manufacture in a market to which exports are no longer possible or feasible, the licensing arrangement serves a most valuable purpose and should certainly be considered as an alternative when direct manufacture has been ruled out for one reason or another. For the purposes of this discussion, it will be assumed that the licensing arrangement has been selected as the alternative to direct manufacture. The comments which follow are intended to cover the various conditions necessary if this alternative is to be a profitable one.

The Market Survey

Just as would be the case prior to reaching a decision to invest in one's own manufacturing facilities, one should make a thorough survey of the market in question before authorizing any commitment to a prospective licensee. This will benefit both licensor and licensee. It will enable negotiators on both sides to evaluate properly the future potential of the rights offered by the licensor and thus to arrive at fair and equitable compensation in the form of royalties or other payments.

The market survey should determine the local availability of raw materials, as well as the necessary skilled labor and technical manpower. It should include a complete study of market potential so that both parties can be assured adequate sales volume which will support economically profitable production in the licensee's plant. A study should also be made of fixed and working capital requirements, and the licensor should satisfy himself that sufficient capital is available, or can be made available from private or government sources, to insure a sound financial basis for the undertaking.

The market survey should reflect sales forecasts for at least five years ahead. Accurate estimates of the licensee's fixed and variable manufacturing costs, including startup, selling, promotional, warehousing, and administrative expense, should result in a fair picture of anticipated pretax operating profits over these first five years. Further negotiations can then take place in an atmosphere of mutual confidence which will ordinarily permit the parties to reach an agreement that will be considered reasonable by both sides.

Evaluation of the Rights

An evaluation of the rights which the licensor has to offer and which the licensee wishes to acquire should, of course, go hand in hand with a thorough market survey as the first steps in preparing to negotiate the payment provisions of the license contract.

Basic patents are presently so rare that the principal U.S. licensing export nowadays is the know-how that does something with basic ideas which may or may not be patented. Even when basic patents do appear, they normally involve considerable technical know-how in the form of so-called "trade secrets" which are indispensable to the licensee. Under these circumstances, it is the know-how and the technical data which should be evaluated as much as, or more than, the patent itself—if a patent is indeed at stake.

Unfortunately, however, know-how and technical data are extremely difficult to evaluate, and very few licensors are in the enviable position of being able to quote a firm "price" for their licensed rights. Hence a certain amount of bargaining is inevitable. If it is to result in a price that is reasonable and fair to both parties, a careful advance evaluation of the costs and profit potential inherent in the licensing arrangement is essential. Negotiating on the basis of "what the traffic will bear" can leave the licensee with no margin of profit or with insufficient financial incentive to exploit the licensed rights. Alternatively, inadequate preliminary evaluation of the rights can result in royalty and other payments that are too low to cover the minimum costs of implementing and maintaining the agreement.

To avoid either extreme and to bolster its own bargaining position, the licensor should have a fairly definite idea of the price it can ask for its rights: a price that is reasonable to both licensor and licensee—that is, which the licensor can reasonably be expected to receive and the licensee can reasonably be expected to pay.

Many variable factors have to be considered in arriving at a reasonable evaluation of the rights being offered. Certainly the following should be taken into account:

+ The patent or trademark position in the local market.
+ The exclusive or nonexclusive character of the rights.
+ The capital investment required on the part of either or both parties.
+ The reciprocal license rights, if any.
+ The going rates for similar products or in similar industries.
+ Competitive offers from rival licensors.
+ The risks involved in disclosing secret or special know-how.
+ The profit life of the know-how and technical data, with or without continuity of replenishment.

PAYMENT PROVISIONS

Once they have estimated the licensee's profits on the venture and arrived at a fair evaluation of what the licensee is "buying" from the licensor, both parties can turn their attention to the most important part of the negotiations: reaching agreement on the remuneration that the licensee will pay for the licensor's property rights—or, in other words, the payment provisions to be included in the licensing contract.

At this point it should be mentioned that there are no true guidelines to be followed. The payment provisions finally agreed upon are almost certain to reflect the bargaining skill and bargaining position of the licensor, as well as the interest of the licensee in securing the rights and his willingness to pay for them.

Initial payments. Despite the licensee's obvious reluctance to make an initial or "down" payment, one should always be included in the licensing agreement wherever negotiations permit. This initial payment, to be made at the time of signing the agreement if at all possible, should be sufficient to recover out-of-pocket expenses in negotiating the license contract and the anticipated costs of maintaining and servicing it. In the first instance, these include such obvious items as the market surveys undertaken, visits by licensor personnel to the licensee's country, the cost of taking care of visiting licensee personnel during their stay at the licensor's plant, and legal expenses connected with drawing up the final contract. Another cost factor to be considered is the expense of providing the licensee with blueprints, manuals, specifications, technical data, and the like. Still another is the expense of filing and maintaining patents in the licensee's country if this is to be done by the licensor.

The costs of maintaining and servicing the agreement should include, if required, the training of licensee personnel, the loan of key licensor personnel, and other technical liaison not covered by specific provisions in the license agreement. Some companies also include a share of the research and development costs for the licensed product or process. However, this is not always realistic since these costs would most certainly have been the same if no licensing arrangements had been considered. R&D is fundamentally an expense incurred to promote the domestic sale of the company's products. It is what makes it possible for the licensor to offer plus values to the licensee. Seldom, if ever, is an R&D program undertaken as a means of engaging in licensing activities.

Apart from its purpose as a vehicle for recovering out-of-pocket expenses and providing immediate income for the licensor, the initial payment serves as a strong performance bond to insure that the licensee immediately uses the license in a substantial way. In those cases where the government of the licensee's country may not approve an initial payment, offsetting arrangements such as prepaid royalties, payment for the transfer of know-how, or an increase in the royalty rate should be considered. On the other hand, where local authorities will approve only low royalty rates, a corresponding increase in the initial payment would seem justified.

Royalties. The principal source of license income will, in fact, be the royalty, which should represent the pro-rata cost of continued research and development (whose benefits the licensee will be expected to share) plus a part of the profit that would have been made from an export sale by the licensor. In many cases, however, the use of this formula will predict amounts in excess of historical rates, and the actual rates agreed upon may then reasonably be lower. Generally speaking, the average royalty a licensor can expect will not exceed 5 or 6 percent of sales, and he may have to settle for less depending on the magnitude of the initial payment, the strength of the patents, and the value of his know-how and trademarks.

When negotiating the royalty rates to be applied to the license, the licensor should be concerned with the *total* price he receives for his licensed rights and services. Moreover, he should consider the overall return from the licensing arrangement rather than any single element of the compensation pattern such as the royalty income alone. It is a high licensing income that should be his objective and not a high royalty rate *per se*. In other words, a coordinated pattern of compensation which will provide the maximum aggregate return in a manner consistent with marketing and management objectives, and which at the same time will not destroy the licensee's financial incentive, should be the aim of the licensor.

A minimum royalty is often desirable as a stimulus to the licensee to develop the market to its fullest potential. Such a minimum has the added advantage of weeding out casual license prospects and those with ulterior motives who have, for one reason or another, no intention of "working" the contract. A minimum expressed as a percentage of approximately one-half to three-quarters of annual estimated sales at the end of the second or third year on the basis of preliminary market surveys is a good rule of thumb to follow. This is usually high enough to induce the desired stimulus yet not impose unfair and impossible conditions upon the licensee.

In the best interests of both parties, there should be provision for reducing the minimum if, after some experience, it is found to be excessive. Also, it may be advisable on occasion to include a carryover arrangement in connection with the minimum whereby excess royalty payments for one period are credited against other periods.

In some cases *maximum* royalty provisions are included in the licensing contract as an incentive to greater production and sales. Or licensors may provide for a descending scale of royalty rates, based on volume, to encourage rapid development of the market and expansion of the licensed operation. Provision for upward or downward adjustment of the royalty rate may, as a matter of fact, result from anticipated changes in market potential, competitive conditions, patent coverage, or any other condition which, in the negotiators' opinion, might contribute to a change in the value of the licensed rights.

The base upon which royalties are to be paid should be agreed upon and clearly stated in the licensing contract. The most usual arrangement calls for periodic payment of royalties as a percentage of net or gross sales. However, the variations in royalty bases are many, including specific rates per item sold, per item manufactured, per item installed, per unit of measurement (that is, weight, length, cubic capacity, and so on). In addition there are royalties figured on annual consumption of base materials. Those that are based on a per-unit rate have the advantage of not being affected by changes in the licensee's costs, prices, selling efforts, or accounting procedures.

Payment for special services. Most licensing arrangements involving technical assistance provide for payment by the licensee for such licensor activities as consulting, purchasing, training, designing, layout work, procurement of material, and the like. Usually, the charge is written on a cost or cost-plus basis and is rarely a large amount.

In instances where the licensor intends to supply components or raw materials to the licensee, there are two distinct points of view which prevail as to their pricing. The first approach is to regard these sales as normal commercial transactions which should be priced accordingly. Proponents of the opposite point of view argue that low or preferential pricing of components or raw materials will, by the resulting beneficial effects on the licensee's costs, insure a greater overall return to the licensor from increased royalties than might be realized from the profits on sales of components and raw materials at the usual markups or at going market prices.

Which approach is adopted depends to a great extent on the nature of the products or processes. In the pharmaceutical industry, for example, the supply of the basic patented ingredient of a specialty, particularly if the licensee is a subsidiary of the licensor, is often marked up several hundred percent as a means of repatriating some or most of the subsidiary's local profits.

Rentals. Rentals normally arise out of leases. However, leases of equipment, which are fairly common in license agreements, are themselves a type of license and should be mentioned at this point as yet another form of compensation to be considered under certain circumstances.

It is considered better practice from a legal standpoint to have the lease part of the overall arrangement set out in a separate document, but there is no legal reason against including it in the license agreement. In this event the lease payments stand by themselves as just one more factor to be included in the overall payment provisions of the contract.

✦   ✦   ✦

In conclusion, it should be stressed that the licensing arrangement is like any other partnership in that it requires a certain amount of give and take on both sides to be successful. The extent of royalty income to the licensor is in direct ratio to the successful efforts of the licensee, and there is no substitute for an atmosphere of mutual trust, sincerity, and conviction.

IV. *A Service*

Robert E. Sibson

M ORE THAN HALF OF ALL EMPLOYEES IN THE UNITED STATES TODAY WORK FOR service businesses. Therefore, the management of such businesses—including the pricing of their services—is of crucial importance, not only to the enterprises concerned but to the economy as a whole.

What is a "service business"? For the purposes of discussing pricing, it will be defined as a business which essentially sells the knowledge or talent of people. Its product is, therefore, what people know or what they do. Either no physical product is involved at all, or it is incidental to the services performed by people.

This definition of "service business" covers a broad spectrum of enterprises. For instance, it includes most financial institutions such as banks, brokerage houses, investment banking firms, and insurance companies. It certainly includes all professional firms such as engineering design specialists, management consultants, public accountants, and law partnerships. The large and growing education field is essentially a service business. Then there are all those entrepreneurs who are essentially providing professional or creative services: doctors, dentists, writers, entertainers, and so on.

ROBERT E. SIBSON is President of Sibson & Company, Inc., in New York City.

Above all, of course, the definition includes most government workers, whether at the federal, state, or local level.

The service business can be a profit-making or a non-profit-making enterprise. It can be in the commercial sector of the economy, it can be in the public domain, or it can be a private institution. So far as pricing is concerned, these variables are not necessarily determining considerations.

It should also be noted that many of the more traditional businesses offering a tangible product have sections, divisions, or departments which are essentially service in nature. A chemical company, for instance, typically has a research division; and this division sells the services of people. All large companies have staff departments at corporate and sometimes divisional levels, and these groups also are essentially providing services. In some organizations, the staff or research services are sold outside the company for a price, as well as inside the company for a cost charge. More typically, of course, their services represent charges against operating profit and loss centers; therefore, the cost allocation of the services represents a price to the operating divisions. In this sense, too, many product-oriented companies have a pricing problem with respect to service activities.

Correct pricing, both in terms of establishing the right prices and in terms of using the right methodology in arriving at prices, is a crucial exercise in any enterprise. In service businesses, however, it is, if anything, even more crucial to success. This is due, first, to the economic structure of the service business. The fact that there is relatively little capital means that pricing and time utilization are the primary elements of leverage in achieving profitability (or whatever criteria of success may be used). Secondly, many service businesses are less subject to the pressures and controls of a marketplace, and hence there can be greater flexibility in pricing policy.

Basic Methods of Pricing

Perhaps because of this inherent flexibility in the pricing of many services, the actual methods of arriving at price number in the hundreds. Furthermore, much of the pricing in service businesses is either intuitive or discretionary, and fixed formulas or methods are frequently lacking.

A recent study of pricing methods indicates, however, that there are six basic methods of pricing:

1. Cost pricing.
2. Competitive pay pricing.

3. Contingency payment pricing.
4. Fixed prices.
5. Contract pricing.
6. Value pricing.

The first task of the service enterprise is to determine, in the light of its particular circumstances, the correct methodology of pricing. In other words, the focus should be not so much on the mechanism or mathematics involved but, rather, on the basic method used. Each of the fundamental methods outlined here has unique characteristics. Each is appropriate under certain circumstances. Finally, each has certain advantages and certain problems.

Cost pricing. The cost-pricing approach is quite similar to traditional product pricing. It is essentially based upon accounting data and arrives at a price by adding up the chargeable cost.

Each of the elements of cost for a given service is determined by accounting methods so that total costs may be derived for various levels of business activity and time utilization. From these calculations a price is then determined which, at the various levels of activity and standard time utilization, will yield a desired profit—or, in the case of nonprofit organizations, will represent a breakeven operation.

This pricing method is used mostly in the nonprofessional departments of professional service businesses. It is, for instance, essentially the type of pricing approach used for the "back room" operations of brokerage houses; some of the support functions in public accounting firms; and, to a certain extent, the nonmedical or hotel services of hospitals.

If we assume that such elements as volume and time utilization can be correctly forecast, the cost pricing system has the virtue of assuring a predetermined profit objective. Unfortunately, accounting practices are not sufficient for the job of accurately identifying cost in many service businesses. Furthermore, there are frequently questions about the proper level of profits for a given service, even in nonprofit activities.

Competitive-pay pricing. What might be labeled the competitive-pay approach is really a special variation of the cost approach to pricing. Briefly, it starts with a determination of competitive or average rates of pay in the labor market for types of jobs utilized within the service enterprise. On this basis competitive rates are then established for the company. Thus the "people" portion of the total cost which goes into determining price is, in effect, determined by competitive rates of pay in the labor market.

This approach tends to be used in government enterprises or in those whose main work is done for the government on a contract basis. In such operations, price is determined by cost; and cost, of course, is largely determined by payroll. The manager of the government enterprise, or the government official who controls cost in a private company doing government contract work, therefore recognizes that to a large extent the rates of pay set for employees determine the price of the service. They also recognize a special public responsibility to control payroll costs. An obvious sign of control—and a superficial way to avoid criticism—is to be certain that the rates paid are average when compared to the rates typically paid for similar types of work elsewhere.

In the absence of a method for valuing the services or products offered, it would appear that, however inadequate, this approach is the only reasonable pricing basis which can be used in government enterprises or in companies engaged to a substantial degree in government contract work. Certainly, men of considerable competence in government agencies, who have addressed themselves to this problem over many years, have not yet been able to find a better way.

The problems with this approach are obvious. First of all, it assumes that valid information with respect to competitive rates of pay is available. While such rates are usually available, their validity is frequently dubious. This is particularly true where the work done and, therefore, the jobs in the government enterprise or the firm doing government contract work are not typical of the work performed by people in other, similar-sounding positions in the marketplace. Competitive pay pricing also is a difficult approach to defend when, in fact, the positions in the government-sponsored enterprises dominate the marketplace. Finally, the competitive-pay approach fails to account for number of people or effectiveness of work, the primary elements of cost in a service business.

Contingency-payment pricing. Still another identifiable method of pricing in service businesses is what may be termed contingency-payment pricing. This approach is essentially the service business equivalent of piecework rates in the factory or commission compensation for salesmen. The fee for services performed is contingent upon a certain act or accomplishment.

Examples of this method are numerous. In employment agencies, for instance, it is typical to charge a fee, based upon a percentage of salary, only if an acceptable candidate is found for a job vacancy and he is successfully placed in it. Contingency payment also is the standard method of pricing in real estate businesses, where the agent receives no compensation whatsoever unless the house is actually sold.

In theory, the contingency system offers the optimum in incentive compensation or motivation to perform. There is a payoff only for successful performance. Unfortunately, however—as many who have opened employment agencies or tried to sell houses have found out—the motivation is to accomplish something in a quantitative sense rather than in a qualitative sense: to fill the job, in other words, but not necessarily with the right person—or to sell the house, but not necessarily at the right price or under the right conditions.

Fixed prices. The fixed-price approach to pricing in a service business obviously manifests itself in a uniform price for a given service in a given area or industry. Many simple legal services—for example, house closings—involve the same fee for all lawyers in the same community. And many hospital services, such as blood tests and EKG examinations, similarly tend to have a uniform price.

This uniformity is sometimes due to a controlling agency such as Blue Cross or to a government regulation. In other cases, uniform pricing tends to result from "agreement" among those who offer the services. If this were to involve large industrial concerns, it would probably be labeled "collusion."

It is difficult to comment upon the appropriateness of a fixed pricing system unless we know the method by which the fixed prices were derived. When we see a fixed price in a service business, we are looking at a conclusion. This conclusion may have been reached by any of the other methods of pricing described here, or it may even represent an arbitrary price established by those who offer the service.

Frequently, of course, the fixed price represents a genuine attempt to protect the public from unreasonable prices for essential services. Experience indicates that this objective may be overachieved; that the resulting prices are so low that they may not even cover costs. This, in turn, means that while part of the price is obtained directly when the service is rendered, part of it must be obtained indirectly from other sources. Examples are college tuition and hospital services.

Contract pricing. Sometimes the fixed price is not just set by agreement or practice but is put in the form of a written contract. For example, there may be reimbursable provisions in contracts covering group insurance. Industry practice or even government regulations may require a written contract.

As in the case of fixed pricing generally, the primary reason for a contract pricing system is frequently the protection of the public at large. There may be an equal advantage to the supplier in that pricing is effectively removed from the competitive scene. The actual and potential problems of contract pricing are, however, major ones; and they could well develop into real economic hazards.

One interesting problem, where the contract prices that are enforced appear unreasonable, is the tendency for the customer to avoid the service altogether. To some extent this is happening today in the brokerage business. Some institutional buyers and the more sophisticated traders are now finding ways to circumvent brokerage fees.

Another danger, of course, is that the administrative mechanisms for changing contract prices can become so archaic that the prices become unrealistically low. This may require that some of the revenues needed to cover costs be obtained indirectly—and in ways which cannot be controlled and accounted for. In other cases it may make it difficult or impossible to provide quality services. This may be particularly crucial if the services in question are essential to the buying public.

Value pricing. The final method of pricing to be noted is the value approach. This system is geared to the willingness and ability of the customer to pay. It is almost the antithesis of the cost approach.

There is a certain soundness in gearing price to worth. Measures of time expended, competitive pay, cost, and the like are, at best, only rough guides to value. Value pricing simply assumes that a new idea, a new and better method, or knowledge which means a great deal to the client should be paid for in proportion to its value to him, particularly where the service is crucial to a broader purpose or the price is a small percentage of the total cost of a larger undertaking.

An example of this kind of pricing is the fees of a legal firm engaged to represent a company in a lawsuit. These fees may amount to $100,000 or more, but if the case is won the company may save millions of dollars. In this instance it is the worth of the service itself rather than the price which is ultimately important.

Value billing is fine, of course, when the buyer has a choice between the services of two or more companies or individuals. However, if there is only one service available—and it is essential—then the value system of billing can get entirely out of hand.

If the customer is a large firm, the price of the service is probably only a small part of the cost of reaching its overall objective. It is something the company must have, so whether it costs a large amount or a small amount is not really vital. However, the customer is frequently an unsophisticated buyer, unable to prejudge the actual worth of a service. Morever, if a service is crucial or essential, how do you put a price on it? For instance, how much is a doctor's service worth if he saves your life?

PRICING AND DEMAND

The various methods of pricing we have discussed occupy different rungs on the pricing ladder, which is structured principally by the elasticity of demand for different services. This elasticity of demand in a service business creates an extremely interesting pricing situation, which varies from the almost completely inelastic to the almost totally elastic.

Inelasticity occurs, of course, when the industry, or individuals within the industry, set a fixed price for a service with no provision for adjustment. At the opposite end of the spectrum, the prices of services are completely elastic, primarily because the buyer has little or no concern with the unit rate per se—generally when the service itself is vital to the individual or the service cost incurred is a minor part of the overall cost of what is being done (as in the value pricing approach).

One thing that enhances elasticity of price under some pricing approaches is the element of time. There can be two elements of price in service work: the daily billing rate and the number of days billed. In truly professional work, the buyer seldom has any idea how many days it takes to perform a given task. Frequently, therefore, the real variable in the cost of the service is not so much the daily rate itself as the flexibility inherent in estimating the total number of days that will be required to perform the service.

Another element which contributes to greater elasticity of price in many types of service businesses is the buyer's inability to measure the quality of the service. In the value system of billing particularly, the unsophisticated buyer has a great deal of difficulty in knowing the right answer when he hears it.

Some people who engage professional services think only of price. Many others, however, think that there are no real bargain prices in this area; that, unless a service is of the highest professional quality, it is usually not worth any price. In fact, a low price may in the long run involve enormous costs if incorrect or bad advice is given.

EXPENSE VS. INVESTMENT IN PRICING

One of the mistakes frequently made in the pricing of services is to consider only the time actually spent by an individual while performing the service itself.

For example, if an investment banker or a lawyer were to charge only for actual time spent in looking at a specific problem and giving advice or rendering an opinion on it, from the commercial point of view he would, of course, be underpricing his services. He would not be charging at all for the knowledge which he must first have acquired in order to perform the service requested—not to mention the continuing time investment in staying abreast of his field or developing new answers and methods.

The acquisition of knowledge is as much a function of cost in the service business as the time spent using that knowledge. If this factor is not taken into account, a business may soon find itself in financial trouble. Failure to include investment time in pricing could ultimately lead to the mistaken belief that the firm could no longer afford the necessary time for research and the acquiring of new knowledge—so that eventually the well would run dry.

When a service business runs out of *knowledge,* its services are no longer of value.

FUTURE TRENDS IN PRICES

One of the problems in managing a service business which has a direct price implication is the inability to apply the usual measures for increasing income in the face of rising costs—particularly rising payroll costs.

Generally speaking, most service businesses do not lend themselves to increased mechanization or automation to a sufficient degree to offset spiraling prices due to rapidly increasing technology and pay rates. Nor do they lend themselves to large-scale operations which theoretically, if not in fact, contribute to greater financial efficiency. To a significant degree, rather, service businesses are inevitably geared to the pace of the human being, which cannot really change. Actually, as the various disciplines of the service business become more complex, the time involved in arriving at any particular conclusion, or performing any particular service, tends to increase.

To cite only one example, the relatively simple process of pulling a tooth requires more time today than it once did. Why? Because not only the patient's expectations but the dentist's methods and skills have changed over the years to demand the use of X-rays, anesthesia, and other new technology.

Sometimes the service requires a fixed interval of time. A classic example is the economic problem faced by a large symphonic orchestra. It takes the same amount of time to play the Beethoven *Fifth* today that it did 150 years ago. Efficiency can't be improved by playing it faster!

This combination of factors will very likely lead to more rapid price increases in service businesses than in product businesses.

METHODS FOR INCREASING PROFITS

Here are some suggestions for the service business that is feeling the economic pinch. These can be taken to either lower cost or increase price —or both.

+ *Build profitability through the value system.* Many service businesses have moved in this direction. The key here, of course, is to build great professional competence and develop proprietary knowledge and skills.

+ *Sell someone else's services at a profit.* This method is almost a tradition in some businesses, such as public accounting and consulting. The firm may, for instance, hire an accountant for $50 a day and bill his services at $125 a day. The more business for $50 accountants, the more profit for the firm.

+ *Transform a professional service into a product.* This involves utilizing the talent of a professional person working on a problem common to many. The answer evolved (and it may be possible to come up with one by programming the problem into a computer) becomes a "packaged plan"—a product which can then be sold. This assumes, of course, that there are a lot of identical problems which can be solved with one answer.

+ *Broaden the market or audience for the service through mechanization.* This can sometimes be done—through television and radio, for instance—even though the service itself cannot be improved by mechanization. (While the Beethoven *Fifth* cannot be played in appreciably fewer minutes than its composer intended, it can be played to twice as many persons per minute.)

In this way, it may even be possible to lower the unit price while at the same time increasing profits.

✦ *Identify the elements of the service which can be performed at a lower level of skill.* People at this skill level can then be hired, at a correspondingly lower level of pay, to perform this part of the service. Hospitals are one example of a service business which employs this technique to some extent—although costs and prices continue to soar. Nurse's aides, for example, take over the less professional duties of the trained nurse. In the same way the general practitioner diagnoses and cares for ordinary illnesses while identifying the more difficult for specialized medical care.

Each of these ways of increasing profits suggests a very different strategy for growth. Not all can be applied to every type of service business. The method chosen must be a function, not only of the kind of service offered, but of the kind of image the business wishes to present.

Special-Situation Pricing

I. A New Product

Richard J. Steele

O F THE SEVERAL THOUSAND NEW PRODUCTS INTRODUCED EACH YEAR, REMARK-
ably few recover even their development costs. This fact will not
surprise most readers. It has been convincingly documented in several recent
studies. Most of these studies are preoccupied, however, with the high failure
rate itself; few of them probe at all into the more important question of why
new products fail.

Many fail because they lack the features desired by the buying public, or
because they are not seen by the public at a time and place conducive to a
buying decision—"the wrong product at the wrong place at the wrong
time." Quite a few fail simply because they have been priced wrong, however, and the error can as easily be in pricing the product too low as in pricing it too high.

This high incidence of new product pricing errors is not hard to understand. New product pricing is one of the few areas of management in
which there is virtually no organized body of knowledge based on practical
operating experience. There is a wealth of abstract economic theory on pricing in general, but it is too far removed from the realities of new product

RICHARD J. STEELE is Vice President, Fry Consultants, Inc., in Chicago.

introduction to be of much help. When the marketing executive faces his first experience in pricing a new product, he thus finds himself relying almost entirely on his own intuition. Even those who make new product pricing decisions frequently report that their success ratio does not improve appreciably with experience.

PRICING AND LEVEL OF NEWNESS

In considering how new product prices actually are set, we must recognize that there are several levels of "newness" and that a somewhat different approach is used at each level.

"Functionally identical" products (Class I). Some products are new only in the sense of being an offering by a new company of a product already established in the marketplace. The new electric typewriter, the new toothpaste, and the new cigarette brand all represent new products of this type. We shall call these Class I new products for convenience.

Pricing such products does present some problems, but the final price is almost completely dictated by one easily determined factor: the prices of functionally identical products already on the market. A new cigarette brand, for example, is unlikely to be priced more than a cent or two above or below similar cigarettes already on the market unless it is intended for a very specialized market segment—perhaps the "snob appeal" market.

"Functionally similar" products (Class II). Other products are new to both the offering company and the market, but are directly competitive with established products which perform essentially the same function. Fiber-glass boats were once in this category, and an electric automobile would be such a product today. These we shall call Class II new products.

Pricing products in this class is more difficult, but even here the established pricing of functionally similar products is a strong consideration. The price of an electric automobile, for example, must be above or below that of a gasoline automobile by an amount that the buyer can rationalize through perceived differences in function or utility. If the electric automobile will not go as far or as fast between rechargings as a gasoline automobile, buyers will not be willing to pay as much for the electric model. Buyers are not always completely rational, of course, in attaching specific dollar values to perceived differences in function, utility, or appearance. Nevertheless, established prices of functionally similar products do establish a clear point of departure in pricing products at this level of newness. Because this standard of comparison does exist, market studies often can be helpful in determining how much of a differential buyers would accept for the changed features of the new product.

"Functionally unique" products (Class III). The most difficult pricing situation occurs with what we shall call a Class III new product—a product which is truly unique in the market, functionally dissimilar from anything seen heretofore. In this class, prices of directly competitive or functionally similar products are not available as standards of reference. Typically, pricing decisions for this class are further complicated because

+ The size of the market for the new product may not be known with any useful precision.
+ No other product or company is likely to have an established competitive position.
+ Customer expectations with respect to services and collateral conditions of sale probably are uncertain.
+ Channels of distribution and discount structures probably are not established.
+ The cost of producing the product may not be fully confirmed.

Thus the pricing decision must be made almost in a vacuum.

Products so completely novel are rare, particularly in the consumer goods field. The first television set was a reasonably good example, but to a degree it overlapped radios functionally. In industrial goods, and especially in areas where technology is advancing rapidly, unique products are somewhat less rare. The laser is one of the more recent illustrations. Even in this field, however, the majority of new products fall into one of the two categories described earlier. Therefore, most marketing executives face the problem of pricing a truly unique product once or twice in a lifetime, if that often.

Even so, it is worthwhile to consider this type of pricing problem quite carefully, because mastery of the approach used in this case will improve pricing decisions for less unique products as well. Particularly if the marketing executive wants to avoid the "me-tooism" of following established pricing patterns when introducing new products, he is more likely to be successful with an unconventional pricing strategy if he plans systematically rather than depending on wild hunches.

How, then, does one go systematically about setting a price for a totally new product? A fairly logical procedure can be described, but only after a few cautioning remarks.

Limitations of the Systematic Approach

The systematic approach is not a magic formula which will lead unhesitatingly to the one price that is best for each new product. On the contrary, a point is reached sooner or later in every new product pricing situation in which certain risks are recognized that cannot be entirely rationalized. At that point, management judgment, intuition, or just plain guesswork must take over. No procedure can eliminate these risks entirely, but a systematic approach can considerably narrow the area of uncertainty. And, looked at broadly, exercising good judgment when all unnecessary risks have been reduced or eliminated is the most important skill of the highest-paid top executives. In the final analysis, it is knowing when to take a chance or when to make an unconventional decision that differentiates the exceptionally able manager from the average.

The approach is outlined here as a logical series of sequential steps, because this is the clearest way of describing what needs to be done. In practice, however, the logic and sequence of the approach are not so easy to observe. In any given situation, some steps may be skipped; there may be backtracking to certain steps (even several times); or the procedure may be carried well along, only to be dropped and started again from the beginning. Therefore, the suggested sequence is offered as a general guide, not a worksheet type of approach.

Also, new product pricing is not something that one can do successfully as a discrete step toward the end of the new product introduction program, just before the first market announcements. Rather, as will be apparent in this discussion, it is a process which must be going on throughout the entire development and introduction of the new product. Decisions which are integral to the pricing process are among the first decisions concerning a new product and also among the last. For this reason, a description of the new product pricing approach is not unlike a description of the entire new product introduction procedure.

Types of Information Needed

The executive pricing a new product must take into account essentially three principal types of information:

1. Why the new product is being introduced and what is expected of it.
2. Legal and marketing considerations affecting price.
3. Product cost.

Product objectives and specifications. Most mistakes in new product pricing can be traced to the first step of the process. It is critically important that real thought be given at the very outset to the questions of why we want a new product and what we want to do, for the short range and the long. Usually there is at least a vague idea that the new product will somehow enhance profits, but that rarely is a sufficient answer. How much profit do we expect the new product to generate, and when? Furthermore, almost all new products are introduced to do more than merely generate profits. Additional objectives may be any of the following, singly or in combination:

1. *To fill in or broaden a product line, thereby enhancing sales of already established products.* Introducing several new package sizes and product sizes of Kleenex, an established product, is a good example. Several automobile manufacturers also have filled in their lines aggressively.
2. *To utilize idle productive capacity in the plant.* This is a particularly popular objective in companies with job-shop factory operations. One foundry, for example, developed a line of trailer hitches which could be made whenever it was not busy.
3. *To iron out a difficult seasonal sales pattern.* For instance, one manufacturer of lawn furniture (a summer item) added doll furniture (with peak sales in December) primarily for this purpose.
4. *To utilize established marketing channels more fully.* An outstanding illustration of this is the effort of the large petroleum companies to utilize their service-station outlets aggressively for tires, batteries, and other accessory merchandise.
5. *To invade a new market or broaden the company's position in an existing one.* A supplier of raw materials to the construction industry recognized that his position was unnecessarily limited and vulnerable, so he became a manufacturer and distributor of a wide line of building products made from these and other raw materials.

6. *To strengthen the company image.* Certainly, introduction of the Javelin by American Motors is a move made principally for this reason.

7. *To sell related or complementary products.* Gas and electric utility companies regularly pursue this objective. Because it is extraordinarily difficult to sell gas and electricity per se, they put great stress on introducing and merchandising new appliances which consume significant volumes of these energy sources. Similarly, Polaroid cameras are merchandised aggressively not so much for the profits they generate themselves as to stimulate profitable sales of Polaroid film.

8. *To exploit an obvious market need.* The transistor is an outstanding example, as was the introduction by Du Pont of Corfam as an alternative to leather.

An effective pricing strategy can be developed for any one or any combination of these objectives. It is critically important to know which is being pursued, because a pricing strategy highly appropriate to one objective may completely block another. If the product is being introduced principally to fill productive capacity, for example, it may be enough for the selling price merely to cover variable costs. A low-price strategy might be disastrous when adding a product to fill in or broaden a product line, however, if the other products in the line were established in the market at premium price levels. Aiming too aggressively at a portion of the low-priced automobile market, for instance, may have done substantial long-term harm to the American sales of a prominent European manufacturer of prestige automobiles.

When the purposes of the new product have been spelled out clearly, then and only then should basic design parameters be established. If this is done before product objectives are set, as often happens when the research and development group charges ahead without adequate marketing inputs, we almost inevitably end up with a solution looking for a problem. Good new product programs are based on products designed to meet a specified market or marketing need, not the converse.

This is a particularly difficult sequence to enforce in companies that are highly technical in their orientation. When a multimillion-dollar company has been scratched out of bare rock by a scientist or engineer starting with nothing but the germ of a technical idea, it is exceedingly difficult to convince that man later that he is not continuously omniscient in conceiving and selecting new products. Yet sustained success in marketing new products requires the closest collaboration between engineer and marketer. If a product is launched for which the market is really not ready, pricing policy rarely will make the product a success no matter how brilliantly it is designed—an elementary dictum which is repeatedly ignored.

On the other hand, the marketing executive should dominate the specification-setting process only in the broadest sense. He should remember that each additional design limitation or requirement tends, as a rule, to add significantly to ultimate product cost. Therefore, overspecification should be avoided. The marketer should confine himself to describing the intended product function, the target market, and only those product characteristics which are known to be absolutely essential to meeting the defined product objectives. Technical design details should be left as far as possible to those most skilled in developing them: the research and development specialists.

Key legal and marketing considerations. A second major area in which information is needed covers a wide range of legal and marketing considerations. For example:

1. *Legal and regulatory factors.* Do we have to give special attention, in connection with this product, to such laws as the Sherman, Clayton, or Robinson-Patman Acts; to special industry regulations, such as building code restrictions in the case of building materials or purity and effectiveness regulations in the case of food and drug products; or to union resistance to a number of products?

2. *Products or services which would compete directly or indirectly with our new product.* How are they priced and marketed?

3. *Probable competitive reaction.* When are suppliers of competitive goods or services likely to react, in what way, and how much will this cost them? Will their reaction be based on a fairly accurate knowledge on their part of our product and marketing costs?

4. *The customer's probable understanding and acceptance of our product.* How novel will the product idea be to him? What advantages and disadvantages is he likely to perceive, and how important will they be to him? Is the buyer likely to be aware

of our product and marketing costs, and can he exercise any control over our cost-price relationships? How sensitive is his demand likely to be to our price?

5. *Probable product life.* Will we have any meaningful patent or trade-secret protection? With or without this, how vulnerable will the product be to technical obsolescence?

6. *Our existing market coverage and image.* How well suited are these to the new product? Will there be any major problems which will be expensive or time consuming to overcome?

7. *General economic conditions.* Are we in a phase of the business cycle favorable to new product introduction in our markets?

8. *Reversability of our pricing decision.* Once we have publicly announced our product and its price, how difficult will it be to change price or marketing strategy? How much are we likely to lose, before we can back off, if we are wrong?

Product costs. The third major area in which the executive making new product pricing decisions needs as complete an understanding as he can get is that involving the costs of launching the new product. He should understand, however, that these costs are pertinent only in establishing a lower limit below which the product cannot be offered profitably. Except in a few highly specialized markets (for example, selling to the U.S. Government), the buyer is concerned only with what the product is worth to him and is totally disinterested in what it costs the supplier. Therefore, a cost-plus approach to new product pricing seldom is realistic. On the other hand, there is little point in offering a new product which must be sold below cost unless this is done for image building or other purposes important enough to justify the loss.

The most frequent error in estimating costs is to consider only manufacturing and direct selling costs and to overlook such additional costs as these:

1. The cost of capital invested in plant and in research and development.

2. The cost of building and carrying inventories, particularly if the product is to be leased instead of sold.

3. Other costs of physical distribution, such as freight, warehousing, material handling, and record keeping.

4. Packaging costs.
5. Costs of carrying increments in accounts receivable and of providing other working capital.
6. Service and warranty costs.
7. General and administrative expenses.

These costs are frequently stated in terms of a set total cost per unit sold. Since the relationship between volume and each of these costs usually is not a constant ratio, however, it is more revealing to construct separate charts of the cost/volume ratios for each cost item, so that a more thoroughly analyzed composite cost/volume curve eventually can be developed. Some of the more sophisticated analysts go one step further and assign confidence ratings to each of their estimates.

SETTING THE PRICE

With information gathering completed, the price-setting executive is ready to start closing in on a pricing decision. Several different patterns of reaching such a decision are popular today. Probably the most common approach is the "seat of the pants" technique. Even if the executive has done a thorough job of information gathering (and frequently he has not), he merely sits back, views the facts arrayed before him, and moves more by instinct than design. There is no pretense of real analysis or weighing of alternatives. Unfortunately, the more sophisticated approaches about to be described are not consistently and markedly superior to seat-of-the-pants pricing, so it is hard to be highly critical of it despite its obvious crudity.

The next higher level of sophistication involves the development of a true marketing plan. Rather than viewing pricing as an isolated problem, the executive following this approach looks at price as only one of several variables which interact to determine product success. Consequently, he develops several alternative marketing plans for the product, satisfies himself that all the variables are structured to act consistently in each plan, and then selects the plan which appears to offer the best overall chance of success, however defined. The pricing decision emerges as only one of several interrelated decisions made concurrently. This approach, obviously sounder than the seat of the pants, is the one insisted upon by more astutely managed companies today.

The most sophisticated approach in contemporary use is based on advanced mathematical analysis, drawing particularly on probability theory. Here, too, price and the other major marketing variables are treated concurrently, but the approach goes further than the marketing-plan approach by defining in mathematical terms the precise interrelationships between the variables. For example, the relationship between volume and variable manufacturing cost is expressed as a mathematical equation, and the reliability of that equation may even be specified mathematically if desired.

The feasibility of this approach depends upon the availability of an electronic computer at this point. All the collected information is loaded into the computer, and the computer then literally experiments with the interrelationships of the variables until it is ready to indicate the relative likelihood of success of all the marketing (and pricing) strategies it has been asked to examine. As with all computer techniques, the reliability of the results depends entirely upon the accuracy of the data and the competence of the instructions fed to the computer.

The mathematical approach has not yet proved itself sufficiently to have found wide use in pricing. Undoubtedly it will do so in the not distant future. At the moment, its greatest value lies in demonstrating more clearly the interrelationships among the variables integral to every marketing plan. Thus it can be of real merit as a prelude—an exploratory step—before developing a marketing plan through a more conventional approach.

THE OUTLOOK

Pricing theory is getting substantially greater attention today than ever before, particularly among specialists in mathematical analysis. New insights are being developed regularly, and the skeleton of a cogent and realistic theory of pricing is beginning to emerge. In the most difficult pricing situations, however, and particularly in new product pricing, it looks as though the competent marketing executive with a good instinctive feel for the market will continue for some time to be of more immediate and practical value than any formalized techniques now on the horizon. Were it otherwise, most of the real excitement of new product introduction also would be extinguished.

II. *A Supplier's Product*

Michael J. Loftus

S UBTLE CHANGES WHICH ARE TAKING PLACE IN THE MARKETPLACE TODAY HAVE short- and long-range implications for buyers and sellers. Distinct trends are affecting not only the marketplace itself but also the *where, when, how,* and *who* of buying and selling. One of these trends is toward longer-term relationships which narrow down the number of suppliers; another calls for contracting annual requirements, which means that a seller gets only one crack at a buyer's business; while still another has to do with the price pressure kept on domestic sellers by those buyers increasing their purchases in international markets.

These changes are taking place partly because the determination of seller's price that used to take place during face-to-face discussion between seller and buyer now occurs back at headquarters, where market intelligence is analyzed and decisions are made. One sees few sales representatives today who can make all the necessary decisions when face to face with a buyer.

The important buying decisions have changed, also. More and more is being done in prepurchase planning sessions involving specialists from

MICHAEL J. LOFTUS is Corporate Purchasing Manager at Brunswick Corporation's General Offices in Chicago.

every discipline. The information explosion is feeding back data from the marketplace in unprecedented quantity and quality. Both buyer and seller are better informed, and their companies are more sophisticated about running their businesses.

But it is not only this speed-up of information that is changing the marketplace for buyers and sellers—the $30-billion race to the moon is having its effect. There has been a fallout of scientific techniques, and the resulting infusion of science into management is affecting the way in which buyers and sellers do business with each other.

FAVORED POSITION OF THE BUYER

The new techniques seem to favor the buyer. Many are analysis-oriented and use mathematics, requiring figures to plan with. And, while the seller has only vague, indefinite figures created from forecasts with infinite variables, the buyer has known production goals and objectives which supply actual, concrete figures.

Examples of techniques being used by buyers today include mathematical decision making, economic modeling, quantitative analysis, linear programming, improvement curves, target pricing, input-output analysis, life-cycle costing, systems contracting, value analysis/value engineering, and preprofit planning through value control. Some of these are not new; they are just more prevalent now than they used to be. Improvement curves were invented in the 1930's. Value analysis was born out of necessity during World War II; it worked and was polished as a purchasing technique at General Electric in the early 1950's. Value analysis of people and tasks, as well as materials and equipment, has led to preplanning for profit through value control. More than one company has been turned around through its application.

Such techniques of forecasting as the Shiskin method or regression analysis aid in sales planning, but that doesn't help the seller in making his presentation or negotiating price. The implication is that buyers have more tools than sellers. From the standpoint of techniques, yes. But marketing research, based on historical data, is showing that each product line offered by a seller can now be constantly measured for profitability, as well as each item ordered from that line by a customer. So product lines are trimmed or dropped much more quickly than before. The buyer's needs shape the marketplace, but now the payback to the seller and the return on his investment have to be clear and specific or a product won't be offered.

IMPORTANCE OF THE PURCHASING AGENT

There are two principal methods by which companies get products to sell—making them or buying them. When companies make their products, not only knowing the unit costs of production but understanding them and being able to control them will provide the means of protecting a profit margin. For an increasing percentage of every dollar that comes in goes right out again for more materials, equipment, and services. And, when companies buy their products, the percentage is even higher.

In World War II, only 40 percent of the sales dollar went for purchases in companies making their products. During the Korean conflict this share increased to 50 percent, and today it is averaging 60 percent. For companies buying their products it is 75 percent. History shows that in 1850 products were made by 98 percent manpower and horsepower with only 2 percent machine power, but by 1950 the figures had reversed and production was achieved by 2 percent manpower and horsepower and 98 percent machine power. Clearly, machines eat up materials many times faster than men or horses. So, as automation increases, the percentage of conversion costs inevitably goes down while the percentage of material costs goes up.

Who in the company is delegated responsibility for monies invested in materials? The purchasing agent, the buyers—both industrial and resale. Others may successfully perform the functions of stating needs, of expediting, of clerical administration, even of evaluating current prices against current value. But only the purchasing agent can deal effectively with the continuing relationship of value to a pricing system.

This is a salient feature in an industrial society where the buyer/seller relationship extends over long periods of time. Nothing is more necessary to the purchasing agent than his insight, his knowledge, his competence, and his recognition as an authority in the field of pricing and sourcing. His success depends on his understanding of pricing policy, pricing tactics, price strategy, and price economics; and he must also be expert at developing sources.

PRICE: THE CENTRAL MEASURE

Some purchasing people have been apologetic about emphasizing price. Many sales people use the term "price buyer" as a form of severe condemnation. Of course, everyone agrees that price alone means little or nothing; emphasis on price to the neglect of other factors is shortsightedness in the extreme. Yet, when all other considerations have been provided for, no item is a good buy unless the price is right.

Price must always be the central measure in purchasing if we are to have a free economy. Except under artificial restraints—for example, official "guidelines," rationing, price control, or monopoly—price can always strike a balance between the objectives of the two parties concerned. Just how the balance is struck depends on the marketing sophistication, the negotiating skills, and the depth of understanding of these two. If they are both sophisticated and understand each other, there is a good chance for real statesmanship to the benefit of all.

Whether it is a question of buying for resale or buying for manufacture, there is a commonality of motive. "Buying for profit" is the key phrase. Since both offer and acceptance are involved in the committing of dollars, it is important to be able to determine the "reasonableness" of a price offered by the seller.

The resale buyer. In the past it was convenient for the resale buyer to be concerned only with what he could sell an item for, so he usually started with his price to the ultimate consumer and worked back from there. He had to get his profit, his average markup, his volume and coverage, because all this measured his performance and, therefore, his salary and bonus. The convenience came in when the resale buyer just took any price offered him and simply marked it up as necessary.

This method led to an easy business relationship with suppliers who understood, when a resale buyer told them he wanted to sell an item for a certain dollar figure, that they must adjust their price, quality, and service to accommodate that selling price. But now there is a profit squeeze and more and more buyers are venturing into international markets in a search for different products or more competitive product prices, dealing with untried suppliers who must be taught from scratch. Thus it is imperative that resale buyers understand the elements of cost that go into a supplier's price and that they specify how much quality, what materials, how many labor hours, how much inspection, what kind of packaging they want.

The industrial buyer. Industrial buyers have used two popular approaches for determining the reasonableness of a supplier's price. One approach, probably introduced by private industry, is to build up your own in-house estimate of what items should cost in the market or would cost your company to manufacture. In small companies the purchasing agent may do this by himself. In larger companies it may involve specialists from design engineering, tool engineering, quality control, production, cost accounting, and purchasing.

Another approach, probably introduced by the government's defense procurement officers, is to apply the techniques of price/cost analysis. The Federal Government has been, of course, the largest single buyer in the world; and considerable legislation has been enacted to protect the taxpayer's money spent for materials, equipment, and services. This combination of buying power and legislation has opened the books of suppliers to price/cost analysis if they want to supply the government; moreover, the techniques that succeed for government procurement, particularly in defense, get passed on to contractors. The upshot has been to condition industry into accepting the techniques used and to make more and more buyers proficient in applying them.

Sharing Information on Costs

The willingness of suppliers to give the information needed for price/ cost analysis is enhanced by the prospect of a larger volume of business for a longer period of time. The idea of a buyer's putting more eggs in fewer baskets often is very attractive to a supplier who wants to stabilize his production, minimize his costs, and maximize his opportunities with less risk. As for the buyer, if he protects himself against such emergencies as fire and strikes, he will do no worse than optimize his position and will probably maximize it. A closer relationship between buyer and seller is required since confidential data must be divulged concerning labor, material, burden, profit, and other cost elements that help make up the price to the buyer. But, when dollars are high and the buyer is trustworthy, increasingly the advantage to the supplier is sufficient for the data to be forthcoming.

It is, of course, disturbing to find that a manufacturer doesn't know what his costs are. Take, for example, Supplier A, with whom Buyer B did $1 million worth of business annually. He was quite willing to provide cost information on his product; the only trouble was that he really had no such data. Eventually he retained an accounting firm to install a cost accounting setup for his operation, and the resulting price/cost analysis was very revealing both to him and to Buyer B, who learned that he was by no means accounting for a large share of Supplier A's other product lines, but in fact Supplier A was carrying Buyer B's product by a large amount. Actually

Supplier A would lose $73,000 if he accepted Buyer B's order to furnish the entire line for the coming year.

Once all the facts were known, it was clear that Supplier A needed more money for Buyer B's product. So Buyer B redesigned the product, which enabled him to provide the money. The remedy was very simple and clear, given the necessary cost data, but it would never have been possible without mutual trust and a sincere desire to eliminate the duplication of costs.

This sort of situation is not an isolated instance; it has happened before and will happen again. But it does point up the advantages of price/cost analysis.

THE IDEAL RELATIONSHIP

A word about the delicacies of those close relationships: Corporate bodies, like individuals, mature and achieve wisdom and stature if they have the proper guidance and direction. When a company has been in business for a hundred years and more, certain lessons are learned and relearned by generations of employees. These lessons produce an atmosphere that spills over into areas such as buyers' relationships with suppliers. They may read like platitudes, but they are effective when they govern corporate life for the long haul.

In addition to carefully worded policies setting forth management's intentions as to how business will be conducted, there are such comments as these, from current leaders in one successful company, showing perhaps even more realistically what the buyer/seller relationship can and should be:

+ "One thing we have learned in 124 years is that you never take advantage of someone but what they take advantage of you."
+ "I want this company to be known as a good company to do business with."
+ "Power over suppliers should never be used to drive them to the wall. If you somehow get a supplier backed into a corner where he will get hurt, then I say let him out."
+ "Vendors must make a profit on our company to stay in business. If they don't make a profit, something is wrong—investigate."
+ "Buyers, think of yourself as salesmen of the company's image."
+ "If in doubt, apply the Golden Rule."
+ "Buyers are in an especially delicate position. Be alert to any

situation that upsets the balance position of the buyer; that might be, or appear to be, compromising."

The codes of ethics drawn up by associations of purchasing men state very nearly the same sentiments. Also, purchasing guides and textbooks stress how much buyers depend on their suppliers.

WHAT BUYERS DON'T NEED

There are certain things, however, that buyers do *not* need from suppliers. They don't need a market with artificial stimuli or restraints that are forever manipulating it in the seller's self-interest. There are still those combinations, left from years of association in industry groups and even out-and-out conspiracy, which try the same old strategies of suspending the laws of supply and demand. We still hear of price fixing, the assignment of customers, the division of territories, restraint of trade, collusion, monopoly, reciprocity, trade relations.

Buyers don't need government stimuli and depressants to add to the confusion already existing in the economy. The invisible hand depicted by Adam Smith as guiding the marketplace still appeals to buyers. True, manipulations of the market by private industry gave us recurring cyclical headaches, but attempts by the Federal Government to correct matters by managing the economy only make us understand at times what it must be to trade a headache for an upset stomach.

Recently, for example, the government told one industry that it is permissible for a seller to call his competition and ask and receive the current price being given to certain customers. Then it took the industry to court for that very practice. When the case was thrown out, the government appealed to a higher court. In the meantime the industry can still combine against buyers in its market.

Industry in general doesn't seem to learn, either. Reciprocity—calling it trade relations hasn't improved it—is one of the weakening factors in the market for which industry groups are responsible. The government has had to step in and apply suitable discipline. After pressure not only from the government but from buyers, more and more marketing men have dropped trade relations because it seemed to close more doors than it opened. In fact, buyers' resistance to reciprocity seems now to be universal.

All such strategies are designed to avoid competition, of course, and companies are missing an opportunity when they avoid the competitive fight in the marketplace. This is the only real physical exercise they get. And they *should* fight. When companies are successful, they get flabby.

Most buyers welcome a battle in the marketplace and are quite willing to take their chances there. It is very often the tough-minded buyer who utilizes both old and new techniques effectively so as to win concessions for his company. He obtains price adjustments even in the face of inflation or industry control. Obviously, if there are enough tough, smart buyers like him, an industrywide attempt to increase price can often be defeated.

GUIDELINES FOR BUYERS AND SELLERS

Every time there is a price change on an important commodity, a buyer should ask himself such questions as these:

1. What would have happened to my supplier, and to the industry price level, if he had not changed his price?
2. Was my supplier the leader?
3. If he followed, whom was he following? What did the leader base his action on?
4. Did I influence the supplier's price change? If so, how?
5. What controlled the timing of this price change?

In turn, sellers should

1. Direct their attention to the buyer's needs—that is, the right price, the right quality, the right service—so that the buyer's performance will satisfy his supervisor.
2. Try to make suggestions about the commodity that will improve price, delivery, quality, or function and thereby help the buyer's company.
3. Always "think value" when selling. Try to determine whether use value, cost value, esteem value, or exchange value will best fill the buyer's needs and aim at that.

In spite of the changes in the marketplace, the infusion of science into planning and decision making, and the pressures occasioned by self-interest and amateurish managing, the buyer still sets the price that will be paid. The seller's pricing strategies may be shrewdly planned, but buying value and buying for the life span of the product have shifted the emphasis and the seller hasn't entirely adjusted as yet to the buyer's new needs. Selling is touted to be a science, but it is not. Selling is still an art while buying has become a science.

III. *Intracompany Purchases*

Richard C. Sarset

T HE NEED FOR SETTING INTERNAL PRICES ARISES WHERE RESPONSIBILITY FOR profit is decentralized. Generally, this involves a reasonable degree of decentralization; that is, autonomous operating units with (1) separable sales and costs, (2) operational independence, (3) free access to sources and markets both inside and outside the company, and (4) an intention on the part of management to measure the operating results of both the buying and the selling divisions on an equitable basis.

GENERAL RULES

The rules for buying and selling should be fair to both parties and, at the same time, take the corporate viewpoint into account. In other words, they should support the corporate financial control system by maintaining consistency between company and division interests. The principles laid down should establish *maximum* price but allow for free negotiation between the parties to set lower prices where warranted. Preferably, the

RICHARD C. SARSET is Controller, Amphenol Connector Division, Amphenol Corporation, in Chicago.

policies and procedures should be reduced to writing to avoid more than normal misunderstanding.

Separate functions may be performed by each unit. For example, one division may design, develop, and manufacture a product, while another stocks, picks, packs, ships, and sells it. In this case, prices should preferably allow the producing unit a manufacturing profit and the distribution unit a warehousing and selling profit.

The policies set should reflect the company's business philosophy. No one pattern works for all; each system must be designed to fit particular corporate needs.

THE TWO APPROACHES

In terms of broad, general principles, transfer pricing follows one of two paths. It is based either on costs or on prices which are tied into market conditions.

Cost-based pricing. When transfers are made from or to service centers which are primarily cost centers (as opposed to profit centers), transfers are usually made at cost. Some executives consider it best not to include any profit on transfers so as to maximize the utilization of facilities. Also, many companies use cost as a transfer-price base because it is simpler and they do not feel that bothering with market-based transfer prices is worth their while. They find cost-based pricing very simple and easy to administer, since cost data usually are fairly readily available. Government agencies seem to prefer it in dealing with defense contractors, public utilities, and the like.

Prices arrived at by this method, say its proponents, generally minimize areas of disagreement, since they permit relatively routine processing of transfers. One further advantage that is often cited is that accounting personnel do not have the problem of eliminating intercompany profit in inventories. Or—to say the least—that problem will certainly be easier to handle.

On the other hand, according to a number of executives, cost-oriented transfer pricing has some disadvantages. Among these is the adverse effect that it generally has on the ROI (Return On Investment) of the selling division. Thus it compounds the problems of decentralized profit responsibility. Moreover, some managers say that, far from minimizing disagreement, cost-based pricing often gives rise to more argument; in fact, the determination of what constitutes cost is itself subject to disagreement. With transfers made on a cost basis, they contend, there is little incentive to reduce costs unless standard cost is an integral part of the operating unit's accounting structure.

In practice, several cost bases are used for transfer pricing. These may involve standard, actual, estimated, direct, or marginal costs. *Standard* (or budgeted) costs are considered to provide a better base than actual, but their use ignores variance problems. The disadvantage of using *actual* costs is that they can be loaded with inefficiencies, whereas using *estimated* costs is considered objectionable by some companies as being too "rough." Management may prefer *direct* or *marginal* costs in setting transfer prices; however, this has the disadvantage of not passing on to the buying division all the costs of making the product.

There are those who think that *cost-plus* pricing tends to encourage interdivision business. In one company which uses the cost-plus principle, the "cost" factor is understood to be standard cost—or, in the case of a new product, *estimated* standard cost. The "plus" factor is established annually by the selling unit on the basis of the current year's forecast. The company's fiscal year is the calendar year, and forecasts in considerable detail are required each fall for the succeeding year. Then, on or before April 1st, the selling division establishes its markup on standard cost for use in all intracompany transfers for the 12 months beginning June 1st.

The plus or markup factor is carefully defined by a written policy, which lists all costs (from the corporate chart of accounts) as being either allowable or not allowable in transfer pricing. For example, no selling or marketing expense is allowable, although management recognizes that some marketing costs are in fact incurred, such as quotations, customer service, and published transfer-price lists. Conversely, general and administrative (including financial) costs are allowable, although it might be argued that intracompany business may be simpler to administer than external business.

This particular firm has two plans for its intracompany business: one to cover domestic (U.S.) divisions, which do not pay any license fees to the corporate office, and one to cover non-U.S. subsidiaries, which do pay such fees to the parent in the United States. Transfer pricing for domestic divisions includes engineering expense as an allowable cost, but for subsidiaries abroad it is excluded, since engineering is paid for in royalties. The allowable forecast costs are summarized as percentages of forecast standard cost of sales. An arbitrary allowance of 10 percent of total allowable costs for profit is figured into the transfer price. As an example, assume that 50 percent of standard cost is allowable for transfer pricing; the intracompany selling price will then be set at 165 percent of standard cost: 100 percent for the base cost, 50 percent for allowable costs, and 15 percent (10 percent of 150 percent) for profit. Thus an item costing $1.00 will sell for $1.65.

The company has established a ceiling on transfer prices consisting of 85 percent of the published price for an industrial distributor. If the price computed by applying the approved factor exceeds 85 percent of the price to the distributor, the transfer price used is 85 percent of the published price. The purpose of this pricing policy is to allow the buying division a modest selling profit.

Market-oriented prices. There are generally three bases used in establishing marketing-oriented transfer prices: the discounted market price, the full market price (usually the current market price), and the negotiated market price.

A number of companies use published or established market price less an agreed-upon discount. This discount may be a flat percentage, or it may differ depending upon whether the product line is very profitable for the corporation or perhaps only moderately profitable. The theory behind the establishment of the discount is that it presumably covers expenses not incurred by the selling division, such as selling expense, credit and collection expense, bad-debt expense, packaging and shipping expense, and so on. The discount is generally established by top management. In some companies the percentage decided upon is that offered to distributors; in other words, the distributor price is the transfer-price base.

The advantages of discounted market prices are several: They are relatively simple to administer, little time is wasted on price negotiation, and there tends to be a better utilization of company facilities. One disadvantage frequently cited is that the discount percentage may not be equitable and so leads to disagreements. Also, comparisons with competitors may be distorted.

Many company executives use full, current market prices in establishing transfer prices. These generally assure normal profit to the selling division; in fact, the profit might be considered above normal, since some costs are not incurred. The buying unit's costs are therefore comparable, and there should be less haggling over prices. Government agencies in particular are less prone to argue with transfer prices established in this way.

The disadvantages of using full market prices should, however, be carefully weighed. Oftentimes no such prices are readily available. For example, how should a component (in contrast to an end item) which is generally not sold as a component be priced? Also, marketing prices in some industries are very volatile—which then involves a lot of "wheeling and dealing" on the part of the two negotiating divisions. Published prices may mean nothing if no one actually buys at them, and it certainly would not be equitable to allow the buying division to use a "phony" quoted market price. Finally, a full market transfer price does not recognize that some costs are not incurred by the selling division.

There are two types of negotiated transfer prices in general use: those which are established for extended periods of time—say, one year or longer—and those which are established for each transaction. Negotiated transfer prices are more flexible, and they encourage price concessions during lulls in production. But they do require that time and effort be devoted to negotiating each price, they often generate disputes which harm corporate objectives, and sometimes a strong executive in one division may take advantage of a weaker counterpart in another.

ADMINISTERING TRANSFER PRICES

Some companies appear to operate successfully without established, written policies. As we have said, however, it is generally wise to establish transfer pricing policies and procedures, to reduce them to writing, and to disseminate them to all concerned. This is usually done at corporate headquarters, with the guidance of the top financial people, after consultation with the division heads. The only sure thing about transfer prices is that they will never please everyone 100 percent.

More often than not, it is the finance man who administers transfer-pricing policies. Disputes may be handled by the corporation president, the top financial man, or an appropriate deputy. Other companies may assign marketing personnel, a top manufacturing or purchasing executive, or an executive vice president to the function.

Also, there are special committees and departments whose sole function is to administer transfer-pricing policies and procedures. In some cases, the committees include representatives of the buying and selling units to make sure that their views are clearly understood. In a few cases, transfer pricing is of such importance that an executive committee of the board of directors handles administration and arbitration. In one company which uses a cost-plus system of transfer pricing, disputes are handled by the corporate cost accounting department, since most of the questions revolve around what constitutes cost.

About ten years ago a large automobile company had a special transfer-price coordinator on its corporate financial staff to administer transfer prices and settle disputes. At that time there were more than a half-dozen employees in his department whose task was to resolve disputes. At the present time, however, such pricing disagreements are rare, owing to greater divisional transfer-pricing experience and the establishment of equitable prices, and administration essentially is handled by one person.

Accounting Problems

Intracompany transfers give rise to a number of accounting problems: the elimination of intracompany profit in inventories, the maintenance of separate accounts for intracompany sales and purchases, the determination of the amount of inventory segregated by the selling division on hand at month's end on the books of the purchasing division. Some companies allow reasonable estimates for these amounts, whereas others require rather elaborate records. Interdivisional inventory transfers may be billed twice —once at cost and, later, with the profit element included. And sometimes corporate headquarters may allocate intracompany profits to the various divisions on the basis of the average standard gross margins realized on intracompany sales on the books of the billing divisions.

Tax Considerations

The situation of transfer pricing becomes somewhat more complex where different taxing authorities are involved. To satisfy U.S. Treasury tax regulations, a foreign-based subsidiary of the U.S. company must pay a "fair" price for any goods made by a product division in the United States. Also, if the U.S. parent or product division furnishes services to the non-U.S. subsidiary, the subsidiary must be charged a reasonable price for them.

Section 482 of the Revenue Act of 1954 gives the Internal Revenue Service authority to reallocate items of income and expense between related company units to prevent income tax evasion and to reflect properly the income of the parties involved. If a company tends to rely upon past Treasury Department rulings and its past audit experience with revenue agents, it may be surprised by the current thinking of the Treasury Department.

There are available proposed regulations, recently issued by the Department, which set forth general guidelines on handling transfer pricing. In general, the Department takes the position that the transfer-pricing policies for foreign-based subsidiaries must reflect to the extent practicable an "arm's length" transaction. An "arm's length" price is the price that an unrelated party would have paid, under the same considerations, for the property involved in the "controlled" sale. It is expected, therefore, that a profit will be realized in the transaction, since it would be unreasonable to assume that a sale to an unrelated party would be made without a profit.

There would seem to be three acceptable methods of determining transfer price so far as the Treasury Department is concerned: (1) the comparable-uncontrolled-price method, (2) the resale-price method, and (3) the cost-plus method. The proposed regulations are reasonably explicit. Those companies which either have or plan to have substantial business transactions (inventory transfers and furnishing of various services) between U.S. operating units and non-U.S. units which they control should study these regulations carefully to make sure that their pricing policies appear to comply with the spirit and intent of the suggested guidelines.

Using the Computer in Pricing

Robert E. Good

CLEVER MEN CAN APPLY A COMPUTER TO ANY ASPECT OF BUSINESS. HOWEVER, A manager's judgment about what areas within marketing are ripe for the use of the computer may be aided by increased knowledge of what other firms are doing. In this discussion, we shall examine a single marketing function—that of pricing—as a candidate for computer applications.

OBJECTIVES AND LIMITATIONS

Our concept of what a computer can do is, to a considerable extent, limited by the range of applications to which we have been exposed. Thus examples of how the computer has been (or may be) used in making pricing decisions can be of value in presenting new alternatives for consideration. Examples may also reveal what types of computer pricing applications some corporations have judged to be currently feasible as well as theoretically possible. A grouping of such examples within the single mar-

ROBERT E. GOOD is Assistant Professor in the Marketing Department of the School of Business Administration, Portland (Oregon) State College.

keting function of pricing should provide a convenient and useful framework for discussion.

There are certain limitations in describing computer applications which are not easily avoided. The examples to be cited cannot hope to fit precisely the personal situations of the majority of readers because pricing is not a single-dimensioned activity. Indeed, the ways in which a computer may be utilized in pricing may vary considerably depending on whether the product involved is new or old, of large or small value, intended for the industrial or the consumer market, and on whether the decision is of the long-range-strategic or short-range-tactical type.

A second problem is the fact that, since the particulars of business vary so much from one corporation to the next, too much detail would be dull and meaningless for the majority of readers. The result of this general problem is that, in spite of a growing body of literature on computer applications, companies can rarely find adequate examples or models after which their own applications can be closely patterned. Published accomplishments either are too general or, if detailed, do not fit the structure of the reader's own problems very precisely. Therefore, the discussion that follows cannot perform the function of a "how to do it" manual. It may, however, provide material that can help the reader spot opportunities for computer-assisted pricing in his own immediate company setting.

TYPES OF COMPUTER ASSISTANCE

The computer can be made to serve the pricing function in a variety of ways. First, it may be used to operate *simulation models*. These models may have pricing decisions as their focal point, or they may incorporate price as just one of many variables. Second, the computer may be used to make pricing decisions or, more accurately, to *execute pricing-decision rules*. Third, the computer can aid pricing decisions by performing *specialized analysis* of data that would not be practical if manual methods had to be used. Fourth, the computer can be used as part of a sophisticated *marketing information system* which, in general, may have the effect of improving the amount, type, quality, timing, and usefulness of a wide range of data necessary for good pricing decisions. It may be argued that the definition of a marketing information system ought to include the first three items mentioned. However, for purposes of this discussion the four-part classification may prove useful. The term "marketing information system" will thus be used in a more restricted sense to apply to the gathering, storing, classifying, sorting, and retrieving of data, whereas the other categories emphasize the analysis or utilization of data provided by the information system.

MANAGERS AND MODELS

A carnival atmosphere of magic and glamour often surrounds the discussion of computerized models. To provide perspective, it may be worthwhile to examine what might be called the managerial aspects of model building and use.

As a demonstration of faith in a secular world, the decision to build a simulation model may be without equal, and this is one of many reasons why models are an interesting managerial, as well as technical, phenomenon. The funds needed for the development of a simulation model are often committed without analysis of the sort that reveals tangible economic benefits. Justification of a model, once built, is often not possible in easily measurable economic terms, especially if the model deals with managerial rather than technical problems. It is frequently difficult to assess the extent to which a model is "successful" owing to difficulties in choosing success criteria as well as in measuring performance against established standards. In short, we may be justifiably curious about the benefits that motivate the construction of simulation models in view of the expense and uncertainty that are often entailed.

First, there may be "political" advantages. The department developing a pricing or more general simulation model may gain in a number of ways. For instance, it may come to be thought of as "progressive" by top management. Even more important, however, a simulation model can help in the presentation of plans and requests to top management. Data generated from models can be used as persuasive evidence in support of one's plan or request; or, during a period of unfavorable performance, a model may be used to show that losses are being minimized by following a given policy. Finally, when a suggestion or inquiry is received, the department which has a simulation model is in a position to respond quickly with detailed information about a wide range of consequences that would likely result from a hypothetical policy or action. More adequate responses are possible, also, when external conditions change—as through competitive action.

The decision to build a simulation model naturally carries with it some risks and costs for the managers immediately involved. To build and operate a successful simulation model may require a more intense and prolonged learning experience than bargained for. Managers must learn to describe explicitly the structure of the problem or environment dealt with by the model—a process which reveals, sometimes embarrassingly, what the manager doesn't know as well as what he does. The degree of certainty associated with each phase of his knowledge also is highlighted. Superiors who must evaluate plans and policies supported by a simulation model must become familiar with the model in order to weigh the evidence presented. Users of the model must continuously work on improving and updating it as conditions change; and, in this sense, a model is never really finished. At many points, a model may be able to rely only on the "currently most useful generalization," which has a limited life expectancy.

The manager dealing with simulation models must learn to argue effectively against them. Models are fallible. It is undesirable either to accept one prematurely or to reject it on an emotional basis. Models are subject to criticism at many different points. The variables chosen for inclusion may not be appropriate, the relationships between them may not be correct, the premises and assumptions for a given model run may not be good ones, and the model may not have been adequately validated. Even when the model has a history of great accuracy, the next run could be inaccurate. In fact, it has been suggested that the time needed for a model to gain the confidence of management is exactly equal to the time needed for a model to become outdated and vulnerable to serious error.

A measure of management's faith in a model is the extent to which it looks upon the model as generating decisions versus data which must be regarded as just another piece of evidence. Most simulation models fall into the latter category, and they often generate the most complex evidence with which managers are required to deal. To evaluate such evidence properly requires an understanding of the model itself, the data used as inputs to the model, and the character of the conditions and factors excluded as well as included by the model.

A PRICING MODEL

Our first example of a simulation model having price as a variable is somewhat unusual in several respects. The model was built by a small company rather than a large corporation. The product, an industrial robot, was a completely new rather than an established product. Since fewer than three dozen units had been sold at the time the model was built, there was almost no sales history, and, in general, very few data were available for building a model.

The robot manufacturer, Unimation Inc., had two main problems to solve. First, a demand estimate was needed so that full-scale production facilities could be planned. Second, the probable consequences of alternative marketing policies, including price policy, needed to be examined to aid in the selection of a marketing strategy and program. The forecasting approaches used included a survey (of customers, prospects, and persons who had never heard of an industrial robot), a study of Census of Manufactures data, and an examination of the adoption histories of similar technological inventions. The model that was developed simulated the purchase decision, which detailed interviews had shown to be quite complex.

This simulation model was designed to augment the other forecasting techniques rather than to provide another independent approach, although the output of the model was a prediction of the volume and timing of sales. The model emphasized that actual sales realized would be a function of management's marketing actions, including price policy, as well as market conditions. It also incorporated the notion that it was more fruitful to look at the probable *rate* of product acceptance rather than the pool of "potential" users. Finally, it was distinctive in implying that a market-potential forecast should not be a one-shot effort but should permit management to revise it easily as market conditions or its own policies changed.

Let us now take a very brief look at the general structure of the purchase-decision simulation model with emphasis on the pricing section. It had three important structural features. First, the decision process was characterized as about a dozen hurdles or filters, including awareness, several types of technical evaluation, financial evaluation (that is, price), evaluation in use, and eventual repurchase. Second, the model had a variety of delay factors which affected the time needed to move from one decision to the next. Third, it had feedback which could affect either the delays or the percentage of prospects passing through the decision steps.

Changed marketing policies or competitive activity could affect the model in three basic ways:

1. The *number* of prospects who started through the decision process could be changed.
2. The *percentage* of prospects who passed through each stage of the decision process could be affected.

3. The amount of *time* it took for prospects to move through the various steps to a purchase and eventual repurchase decision could be affected.

The financial-evaluation decision step had the following general rule:

If A is greater than B (where B equals the price of the robot and A equals the labor savings for a given prospect), pass on to the next purchase-decision step; if not, drop out as a prospect.

Labor savings were calculated under 30 possible combinations of number of shifts, payback criteria, and number of workers per shift replaced by the robot. An average industry wage figure plus fringe benefits was used to calculate labor savings. Both census data and survey information were used to establish the percentage of firms having one-, two-, or three-shift operations, the percentage using a one-, two-, or three-year payback criterion for capital equipment expenditures, and the proportion of cases where the robot could replace one or two men per shift.

While any one step in the model could be calculated by hand, the degree of complexity was sufficiently imposing to preclude hand calculations when the dozen steps all were involved. In addition, the model was run through 12 cycles for each simulated year, which made cumulative and feedback effects very complex indeed.

The model was useful to management in a variety of ways. It helped make explicit about a dozen major steps in reaching a decision to purchase an industrial robot. These steps highlighted the barriers of consumer resistance that needed to be overcome by a well-designed marketing program. The effects of alternative prices ranging from $15,000 to $25,000 could be examined in a dynamic sense; that is, concurrently with other changes in the marketing program which could alter the impact of price changes. The effect of price on the speed of market acceptance as well as eventual total sales (that is, a saturated market) also could be examined. The variety and complexity of these types of pricing analyses would not, of course, have been feasible without the aid of a computer. Noteworthy is the fact that in this case a small company, with a scarcity of data and an unusual product situation, was able to utilize the computer to help make pricing decisions.[1]

---

[1] Another type of model deals with pricing as the exclusive focus of interest. For an example of this type, the reader may wish to examine a competitive-bidding model developed under the direction of Franz Edelman for Radio Corporation of America. See Edelman, Franz, "Art and Science of Competitive Bidding," *Harvard Business Review*, July–August 1965, pp. 53–66.

COMPUTERIZED PRICING DECISIONS

Structure is not a natural or given phenomenon but rather an act of individual perception and, not infrequently, a good deal of human effort. Thus it may be only a slight overstatement to say that there are no management decisions that are intrinsically unstructured, only decisions for which managers have not yet decided to make decision processes explicit. The practical implication of such an assertion is that no management decision is beyond the reach of automation. Our purpose here, however, is not to argue the case of an omnipotent computer, for its potential is—fortunately for us—greatly limited by the economics involved. Rather, our task is to examine some types of pricing decisions which can be computer-automated on a practical basis and the process by which this may be accomplished.

The procedures for developing automated decisions can be stated in a general way quite simply. First, the manager must describe in a clear and unambiguous fashion how he actually makes a decision—or how, given plenty of time, he would like to (that is, ought to) make it. To this description may be added operations-research-type concepts of optimal decision procedures and the like. The final decision rules are then programmed and tested before responsibility for actually making decisions is entrusted to the computer.

How are decision rules made explicit in a firm? Decision structure often becomes explicit in an evolutionary way. At the lowest level, decisions are made intuitively and by trial and error. Second, historical precedent and custom may be used as a general pattern. Third, statements of policy may come to be available in the firm for any given type of decision. Fourth, detailed procedures may be developed in which steps to be taken and factors to be considered are described (detailed planning procedures are an example). Fifth, rules of thumb, bench marks, guidelines, and cues come to be recognized and sometimes are committed to paper. Finally, the most sophisticated step is the statement of unequivocal decision rules that are suitable for computer programming.

One dimension, or measure of management sophistication, is the degree to which the firm's problem structure and decision procedures are well articulated and explicit. A firm at the first or second stage of the evolutionary process might have greater difficulty in automating decisions than a firm at the fourth or fifth level. Of course, the rate of evolutionary progress may not be uniform throughout the firm. The marketing department might be very much ahead or behind other departments in this respect.

Many types of computer-automated pricing are possible. One application involves a major downtown department store which has recently expanded operations to include about a dozen suburban stores. This expansion put stress on management. Difficulties were especially acute for the buyers. The alternatives were to assign buyers to each new branch store and thereby increase overhead or to develop an automated information and decision system that would allow existing buyers to handle the substantially increased amount of work. The latter course was followed, and as a result some standard items are now purchased by computer although the buyer still plays a role by providing a forecast input. Of greater interest, however, is the fact that the computer is able to help the buyer spot slow-moving items (defined for the computer by the buyer) from the daily sales reports for some types of merchandise. These items are listed by the computer as suggested items for price reductions or other appropriate action. Prior to programming these simple decision rules, buyers had to identify slow-moving items either by being out on the floor and noticing them or, more recently, by examining detailed reports. Both these approaches were less thorough, took more of the buyers' time, and resulted in less timely decisions than the current automated procedure.

As computer utilities, such as KEY-DATA Corporation in Cambridge, Massachusetts, are able to serve small businesses, the opportunities for automated pricing decisions will increase rapidly. Automated pricing for relatively small independent steel warehouses, for example, will soon be practical. Such an application could be especially attractive because the pricing procedure for each order is extremely complex and involves many computations but, at the same time, is highly structured. Its value would lie in the fact that pricing errors would be largely eliminated and a great deal of tedious clerical work avoided, with a concurrent reduction in labor costs. The invoicing process also could be speeded.

SPECIAL TYPES OF ANALYSIS

The computational power of the computer gives much greater freedom in the selection of methods for analyzing existing data. Among the great variety of statistical techniques, multiple regression and correlation analysis is the best known; however, it has come into widespread use only with the availability of the computer to perform it. This technique has been used by a large food products manufacturer to examine the relationship between price (and price discounts for distributors) and sales volume. Predictive accuracy has been sufficiently high to enable the company to use the results for planning and examining alternatives. A somewhat more novel approach has been to use regression and correlation analysis to examine the impact of competitive price changes on the company's own performance indexes: sales, market share, growth rates, profits, and so on.

This same company has recently been able to achieve greater managerial use of Bayesian decision theory. Important decisions—including pricing decisions—now are frequently structured in a Bayesian context with lists of alternative outcomes, magnitudes associated with each outcome, and subjectively rendered probability assessments. Although special educational programs and the availability of staff assistance have helped to popularize the Bayesian decision framework, the availability of the computer to operate both special-purpose and "canned" probabilistic decision programs also has played an important role in reducing the amount of tedious hand calculation necessary.

Information Systems and Pricing Decisions

An increase in the sophistication of a firm's information system may increase the potential for better pricing decisions. More information does not, however, guarantee better decisions. We might predict that a firm having a well-structured decision system would be likely to benefit the most from an increase in the amount of data available. On the other hand, the firm with poorly articulated decision procedures would be likely to encounter greater difficulty in seeing how a given piece of new data could impinge in a specific way on any given decision. In either case, a data-rich decision should be more difficult to make than a decision for which data are lacking because one cannot, in good conscience, make an arbitrary decision when there is a good deal of relevant data available. Instead, there is a challenge to evaluate the complexities of the situation carefully.

An improved information system can help provide better background information for pricing in a variety of ways. First, an increase in computational capacity may open up new possibilities for gathering data that were not previously feasible. For example, the firm which has had marketing data consisting primarily of performance data like sales, market share, and profits may be able to go further and gather information directly from the customer, on the one hand, and record decision histories or actions on the other hand so that the relationships between actions and results (in terms of both sales dollars and other consumer reactions) can be analyzed. An improved information system may provide data to be processed by an explicit model or directly by the manager in a less explicit way.

An improved data-retrieval system has been an aid in pricing and other strategic decisions for a large consumer goods manufacturer. A great many brands were involved, with little communication between the brand managers so far as the results of detailed research on each brand were concerned. With a new library system, relevant market research done, say, on Brand A and Brand B is coded and made available to the manager of Brand C.

Use of a computer (through a service bureau) has been helpful to Hotel Corporation of America in capitalizing on registration and reservation information. Although evaluation of advertising effectiveness is the most powerful application for this firm, the guest history data have also been used to aid in assigning rooms at a preferred price to "repeat" customers.

A more complex example of an expanded information system which could help in pricing decisions is that of a large electrical goods manufacturer.[2] The marketing manager and the sales manager were frequently required to approve bids proposed by salesmen; and, being far removed from the field, they needed more information to make intelligent decisions. Two principal components of each bid that had to be evaluated were (1) the size of the discount from an industry-established "book price" that was being offered and (2) the delivery schedule.

There were two important justifications for the development of the system. First, it promised to save the company money. Incongruously, engineers were required to submit elaborate analyses for expenditures in excess of $10,000, yet marketing men decided the discounts to be offered in connection with huge jobs on the basis of intuition alone. A discount range of, say, 6 to 16 percent on a $500,000 job might be decided in just this haphazard manner—with the possible result that if a 16 percent discount were given when only a 6 percent discount was needed, $50,000 would be lost. Second, the system promised to help solve production and engineering

---

[2] This system has been designed but has not been implemented since priority in the use of systems personnel and computer time has been given to production systems.

scheduling problems which had become quite acute. The information system would provide a summary of jobs won and, on a probabilistic basis, jobs that would be coming in soon.

No special efforts were to be made to obtain information that had not always been available. Prior to the installation of the MIS, however, much of the information that was available was never recorded—partly, at least, because there would have been no efficient way to retrieve it when needed from the tremendous volume of paper files that would have been generated. Available information consisted of a wealth of details about past bids, won and lost, and about the status of current bidding situations. This was to be used in a variety of ways.

The headquarters salesmen would be able to utilize the information generated by the system to help in their pricing or bidding decisions. By having a history of past successes and failures for a given industry, they would know what average off-book prices were necessary to get a job. Of course, such men have a feeling for this information, but there was a natural tendency for them to think that a bigger price discount was needed than was often the case. The system could help to compensate for this judgmental bias. The actual bid made by the salesman would have to be adjusted from the "average" according to the particulars of the situation—including the individual competitors involved.

The headquarters salesmen would also be helped by the system when they approached the engineering and production departments to get approval of delivery dates. The salesmen would be able to confront these departments with data on how much and what kind of work they had scheduled as compared to the capacity available. The production and engineering information would be handled on a probabilistic basis from "chance-to-win estimates" submitted by the salesmen.

The three sales managers could use the system to tell them how they were doing compared to targets. In the past, many performance measures had been reported very infrequently; now, information could be supplied on sales volume (by industry, product type, customer class, and so on), proportion of outside vendor business, and share of market. The information system could thus facilitate personal performance evaluation on a more complex and accurate basis. Price discount decisions could be made conditional on targets that were being met and those that were not.

The marketing manager, being furthest removed from the field, felt the lack of information most keenly and, when required to approve a bid, would try to remedy the situation by asking many questions of the salesman. Answers to some of these questions were available; others, however, were unanswerable. The marketing information system would make it routine for the salesman to enter on a form many of the pieces of information that the marketing manager usually requested prior to giving his approval of a bid. The system also could provide answers to questions which could not be answered by the salesman.

The following six questions were the ones most frequently asked by the marketing manager in connection with approving bids:

- ✦ *Who is the competition?* The system would be able to show historically what different combinations of design features, off-book price, and delivery dates were needed to win against different competitors in various industries.
- ✦ *What are the results for the last three months?* In order to get an approximation of how big a price discount should be offered, the marketing manager would want to know the recent history of wins and losses in a particular industry and the off-book prices that were offered in both cases.
- ✦ *What is our capacity for additional business?* There would not be much point in bidding an especially low price if both engineering and factory capacity were fully employed. Also, such a situation would offer a chance to raise price levels. If, for example, the company bid 8 percent off book and a competitor won the job by bidding 15 percent off book, the competitor would learn after winning that it had bid far lower than necessary to win.
- ✦ *What is the mix of business on this job with respect to outside vendors?* If the job involved a product that was mostly company-manufactured, there would be more leeway in granting a bigger off-book discount, whereas a large price discount on a product that was mostly vendor-supplied could mean that a loss would be incurred.
- ✦ *What is the performance on targets to date?* The marketing manager might want to vary his criteria for granting approval of a particular job depending on whether he was running ahead or behind on total-sales, off-book, and outside-vendor targets.
- ✦ *Are other company divisions involved?* Special efforts at coop-

eration in pricing might be expected if the job being bid on was part of a system being offered by another division.

If there is a new emphasis in pricing today, it can perhaps be characterized as a quest for data-based and justifiable pricing decisions. Top management is asking these and still other embarrassing questions which exert pressure toward more analytical decision making. In any event, the computer is being used in making pricing decisions by many different types of companies in many different types of ways. The examples we have discussed serve to highlight the fact that there is great latitude in the manner in which a computer can be used to aid pricing. The challenge is to develop a creative and useful application in one's own particular situation; and numerous companies, both large and small, are doing just that.

When a Price
Must Be Changed

J. Sidney Johnson

I F THE ECONOMISTS ARE RIGHT IN THEIR PREDICTIONS THAT WE ARE TAKING OFF on a steady if not rapid inflationary spiral, we will see prices advance, not once, but probably several times in a multitude of products. It is therefore highly important to give careful consideration to how these price increases should be effected and announced by the manufacturers.

Usually manufacturers give a lot of thought to how a price advance or decline will relate to their product's retail selling price and the selling prices of competitive items. However, they frequently fail to consider how the announcement of a price advance will affect the wholesaler or distributor or retail customer. Many times this results in needlessly antagonizing the very people upon whom the manufacturer depends for the promotion and sale of his product.

This is the phase of pricing that will be discussed in this chapter. The examples given will be from the food industry. However, the same princi-

J. SIDNEY JOHNSON is a marketing and trade relations consultant in New York City.

ples apply to the pricing of almost any consumer product sold through wholesale and retail distributors.

THE IMPORTANCE OF TRADE REACTION

Price changes are prompted for two reasons. First, an increase or decline in manufacturing costs necessitates a change in price. Secondly, and more frequently, a price change occurs because a manufacturer either wishes to attract new users, in order to gain a larger share of the market for his product, or feels it is necessary to meet a competitive situation.

These are good and sufficient reasons for changing prices; but too often, in instituting a change, the manufacturer either overlooks or disregards the great importance of trade reaction to it. By giving his customers too little advance notice, or otherwise timing his action adversely, he does great damage to his company image and to the continued sale of his product.

In recent years, price advances have far outnumbered price declines because of the inflationary spiral in commodity prices generally. However, there are certain products, such as coffee, sugar, and flour, which either are basic commodities or require little processing and whose prices can go up or down quite suddenly. Obviously, the manufacturer must be alert to the advance or decline of such products and quickly change his own price structure accordingly. Within these basic commodity groups, it is obviously difficult to give any advance notice, especially of a decline in price. A price reduction invariably attracts consumers' attention, particularly on a product—like coffee—that is frequently purchased. Therefore, the manufacturer will usually wish to protect his brand franchise by being among the very first to lower his price, hoping to attract consumer buying.

In any case, changing a price in either direction is a delicate matter.

GOOD TIMING BUILDS TRADE SUPPORT

Generally speaking, manufacturers are fully aware of the timing problem and its importance. It is amazing, nevertheless, to observe how many of them completely overlook this factor and how ill-considered many of their announcements are. Thus their price changes create sales resistance and lose them the goodwill of their customers, not only when the news is first received, but sometimes for months and years ahead.

Yet it *is* possible to cushion the impact of a price change. Some manufacturers guarantee the prices of package groceries against their own price decline at least for a reasonable period of time; retailers plan their sales activity at least five weeks in advance, but can adjust to three weeks' notice of price changes on commodities that sell in considerable volume. And similar notice of price increases can often be given.

It is worth remembering, however, that the manufacturer may not always be alone in making his change; others may be raising or lowering prices at the same time. Recently three large paper manufacturers advanced prices 20 percent. One of them offered to accept orders at the old price for four days after the announcement if the orders were to be shipped within approximately two weeks. The second manufacturer agreed to accept orders at the old price for shipment within four or five days. The third manufacturer agreed to accept any orders at the old price for two weeks.

The dilemma of the distributor in this case is readily apparent. The manufacturers were trying to be helpful, but he still had to anticipate his requirements and adjust his prices simultaneously on three separate lines of well-known, strongly advertised paper.

How Will This Change Affect the Customer's Profit?

A prime factor in making a price change that is frequently overlooked by manufacturers is the effect that the change may have on the profits of distributors. If the manufacturer's product carries a gross profit of 20 or 25 percent, he should consider seriously whether a price advance will or will not enable the customer to enjoy that same rate of return—provided, that is, he wishes continued support from that customer.

For example, a retailer may make a 20 percent profit when he pays $4.32 for a case of 20 packages which retail at 27 cents each. If the manufacturer raises the price to $4.78 per case, the retailer makes only 17.6 percent at a new retail package price of 29 cents, and 17.6 percent is not an acceptable gross profit on a product that has been returning 20 percent. Yet the retailer will be reluctant to raise his price to 30 cents in order to maintain his previous gross profit on the item.

This sort of concern for customers' gross profit would seem an obvious requirement for manufacturers who hope to stay in business. Just as distributors have conditioned themselves to "think retail," manufacturers must learn to "think distributor."

Deals and Allowances Cause Confusion

In the food industry, price changes during recent years have frequently taken the form of deals or allowances, especially on instant coffee, soap products and detergents, and other fast-moving items. These are short-term declines. The trouble is that, if one manufacturer offers a deal, his competitors act quickly to meet it or to offer an even more attractive deal.

At one chain store headquarters, deals alone make it necessary to change the retail prices on 44 different branded grocery products on a single Monday morning. Each of the manufacturers responsible for these deals anticipated special point-of-purchase displays of his product—a physical impossibility because 44 special display areas do not become available at one time to satisfy manufacturers' requests. Yet, without special displays, deals obviously cannot get consumer attention and are practically worthless.

It is therefore obvious that every manufacturer's deal must compete for retailer cooperation with the deals offered at the same time by other manufacturers. The manufacturer must make his deal or promotion so attractive that it will assure the cooperation he needs in order to make it effective.

"Cents off." One method of announcing a temporary price reduction is the "cents off" label deal. As the shopper moves about the store, her attention is attracted by a specially printed label offering, say, five cents off the regular price of a familiar product. This is a strong inducement to buy, and it often results in volume sales. Overused, however—as it often is—it causes a great deal of confusion.

For example, a package of flour was offered with a promotion allowance of 50 cents per case. This resulted in a reduction in the shelf price from 57 to 52 cents per package. Then the manufacturer came out with a label deal specifying five cents off. It was intended that the regular shelf price of 57 cents be reduced to 52 cents, but what about the 50-cents-per-case promotion allowance? The two reductions supposedly meant that the price must come down to 47 cents and might well have resulted in conflicting prices on the same package on the same shelf. And the confusion, remember, was introduced by the manufacturer himself, not by the competitor.

In another instance, a manufacturer offered an allowance of 25 cents per case of 48's on a dessert powder for a 30-day period; there was to be a count and recount of warehouse stock to determine how much would be paid. The 25-cent allowance on a case of 48 packages was not sufficient to justify a price change for such a short period of time, but the manufacturer could offer extra merchandising support in order to collect the 25 cents per case. The deal did add to the distributor's profit, but it was not very effective in promoting sales for the manufacturer.

Still another manufacturer offered 60 cents per case on canned meatballs as a display allowance which was to be reflected in the retail selling price. He asked for store displays—a highly unrealistic request for a slow-moving item. Would you, as a distributor with a warehouse transfer of 35 cases to 100 stores, be inclined to give display support? Not likely. The allowance failed to pay off.

Utter confusion resulted from a deal offered by a maker of instant coffee. The regular shelf price was $1.23 for the ten-ounce jar. The manufacturer offered an allowance of $2.40 per case, which encouraged the operator to set a retail selling price of 99 cents. Before this deal had expired, the manufacturer made another offer of two ounces free with the regular ten-ounce container. Was the distributor to advance the price on the previous deal back to $1.23, or should he continue to offer the regular 10 ounces at 99 cents and the 10 ounces plus the two free ounces at $1.23? Or what? Distributors were not only confused but irritated and resentful.

Come to any meeting of distributors or retailers and you will hear an angry chorus of accusations about this kind of incident and the extra work it creates.

"Advertise and/or display" allowances. Where there is a cooperative merchandising contract offering payment for well-defined services at the retail level, there is no difficulty in pricing merchandise. The operator earns the allowance by performing the required services. But what of the situation where no such contract agreement exists? The manufacturer reduces his invoice price for a limited period of time, but asks the distributor to "advertise and/or reduce price" or to "advertise or display." Or he makes no specific request of any kind—simply offers the allowance off the regular price.

In all such cases, the distributor is often at a loss to know how to perform. If the offer is limited to a specific time period, as was the packaged-dessert deal, his problems are multiplied. The net result is time and money wasted.

Allotments of deal merchandise. Manufacturers who announce a cents-off label deal or a per-case allowance for perhaps 60 or 90 days often allot the deal merchandise on the basis of the distributor's established sales of the product. At the reduced price, of course, sales may well exceed the allotment which the manufacturer has allowed a particular distributor. The distributor is then embarrassed by having to raise his retail selling price at the very time when a competitor may be offering the same product at the deal shelf price.

What the manufacturer should do, obviously, is to make his allotment and then offer the distributor the privilege of placing at least one if not two additional orders for deal merchandise. In this way he will be able to compete with other distributors offering the same deal in his market.

Duplication of merchandise. In announcing deals or special allowances manufacturers must also consider the effect on the distributor's warehouse stock. If, just prior to the announcement, the distributor has made a purchase of the product in question, the deal merchandise will greatly increase his warehouse stock. Furthermore, the regular-price merchandise may still be in the warehouse 30 to 60 days after the deal merchandise has been sold.

Some manufacturers allow extra dating on the regular merchandise in order to reimburse the distributor for carrying duplicate stocks of the same item during the time the deal is in effect. Even extra dating, however, does not eliminate the problem of warehouse space on the duplicate stocks. Wherever possible, large orders for regular merchandise should be reduced or shipment deferred in anticipation of the announcement of deals and special allowances. Actually, the distributor would like several options: not merely extended dating on his purchases of deal merchandise but the privilege of invoicing the manufacturer for his stock of regular merchandise (which the manufacturer would then invoice back at the conclusion of the deal) or perhaps invoicing the deal merchandise at the conclusion of the deal when it has been shipped to his stores and sold at retail.

Simultaneous notice of deals. Distributors frequently complain that certain favorite accounts are informed of a deal or a price decline before other accounts in the same market. This naturally causes great embarrassment. The situation occurs where the manufacturer announces a deal or a price decline only through his salesmen. Such announcements are better made to all distributors at the same time by mail or telegram. Salesmen cannot possibly contact all their accounts in one market on the same day, particularly in larger markets.

Retail support for promotional activity. What about advertising or promotional support for deals and price declines? Will it be scheduled so that all distributors have the deal or the lower-priced merchandise to offer at the same time? Occasionally manufacturers arrange for advertising in such a way that some distributors benefit while others do not and so are at a disadvantage.

What kind of support will retail salesmen give deals or special allowances? Point-of-purchase displays and the manufacturer's advertising can be scheduled so as to make them much more effective. It is difficult, however, for salesmen to get to all their accounts in the same market far enough in advance to offer promotional assistance to each one.

Short-term deals and allowances have come to replace out-and-out price cuts in the food industry in recent years. Some few manufacturers condemn them, saying they are merely camouflage—not a means of meeting the issue squarely. Others believe that deals and allowances make price declines more palatable; they maintain that the cents-off package deal in particular is more effective than a price decline. It may be true that, for a limited time, this device does attract a consumer's attention to a product, but it should be stressed that constantly repeated deals puzzle not only the retailer but the consumer—who may conclude that the cents-off price is the real one.

In summary, the policy of using deals and allowances to achieve price cuts may not be condemned per se, but the methods used in haste to meet a competitive situation should be very closely examined. Manufacturers tend to forget that the harm done by adverse trade reaction can more than outbalance the benefits expected from the deal or allowance, no matter how attractive it may be. Granted, special deals and allowances create store excitement. They project consumer interest. They whet competition. They are a powerful influence in promoting sales of advertised products. But the utmost care and caution must be used in planning them and announcing them.

THINKING FOR CUSTOMER SUCCESS

It is urgent that the manufacturer think in terms of his customers' success, not simply of his own desire to capture a larger share of the market for his products. Both are important, but in the long run the manufacturer's success will be determined largely by the consideration he gives his customers' problems.

Manufacturers have problems of their own, certainly—the perpetual problems of sharp and changing competition and the constant effort to expand their share of market. And how will they accomplish these objectives? Surely not by irritating and antagonizing their customers by thoughtless, slipshod practices in handling price changes.

Conclusion:
The New Framework
for Pricing

Jules Backman

THE ENVIRONMENT WITHIN WHICH PRICING DECISIONS ARE NOW BEING MADE has changed markedly from that prevailing a quarter of a century ago. Of particular importance in this connection have been (*a*) the intensification of price and nonprice competition, (*b*) the increasing concern with public relations and respectability in pricing, and (*c*) the expanding role of government.

Increasing Competition

Competitive pressures here and abroad have been increasing dramatically. The ceaseless search for new and better ways to produce many goods has contributed significantly to the intensification of such pressures. Compe-

DR. BACKMAN is Research Professor of Economics, New York University.

tition is expanding both from companies already in an industry and from companies in other industries. Sometimes the latter have entered into the production of items already being manufactured. More often they have developed substitute products.

Competition is intensifying in terms of price and nonprice factors. Consider, for example, the test-tube competition in the expanded research laboratories which have flowered in many industries. Although the major research and development efforts formerly were undertaken mainly by the relatively new chemical and electrical machinery industries, in recent years older industries, such as steel, have had to expand their research programs to fight off the inroads of substitute products. Accordingly, the area of competitive pressure is steadily widening.

The creation of *new* companies is a vital competitive force. However, competitive pressures are more typically generated when an existing company expands its product lines either by merger or by the initiation of new activities. The growth of the conglomerate—a company operating in different markets in which it encounters different combinations of competitors—has been one of today's significant developments.

For example, companies based on other industries have moved into chemical markets on a massive scale. Most of the leading petroleum companies now produce many chemicals. Concerns such as Socony, Shell, and Humble have chemical operations as large as or greater than such traditional chemical companies as Stauffer, Rohm and Haas, and Hooker. In addition to these petroleum processors, Borden, National Distillers, Firestone, Eastman Kodak, W. R. Grace, and many others have become important factors in the chemical industry. It is against this background that Dow Chemical has observed: "Whenever we look up, it seems, one more brand-new competitor comes charging at us."

The net result of movements across traditional industry lines has been an increase in the number of competitors, large increases in capacity, and, in some instances, price cutting. The resulting conglomerate has been providing a new dimension to competition. It is particularly important where large resources are required to compete effectively with companies already in the industry. The developments in the computer market are illustrative.

In many instances, substitutes produced by companies based in different industries also have broadened the dimensions of the market. For example, steel containers compete with glass containers, as shown by the efforts of the steel industry to enter the soft-drink market. In fact, the U.S. Supreme

Court recognized the importance of direct competition between these two types of containers in its decision in the Continental Can-Hazel Atlas merger case. Aluminum entered the tin-can market, and the steel industry responded with the development of thin tinplate. And polyethylene has added a new dimension to the milk-container market, traditionally held by the glass industry.

Similarly, in the Cellophane case the Supreme Court refused to confine the market to cellophane. It defined the market more broadly as flexible packaging materials, including aluminum foil, glassine, waxing papers, sulphite bag and wrapping papers, pliofilm, polyethylene, Saran, and Cry-O-Rap. The Court held: "That market is composed of products that have reasonable interchangeability for the purposes for which they are produced—price, use and qualities considered." This is a more realistic definition of a competitive market than one which is limited to a single product and which excludes substitutes. However, in later decisions much narrower market definitions have been used by the Supreme Court.

Innovation has added another new dimension to competition as test-tube competition has yielded an enormous flow of new products. In some industries, the changes have been dramatic. For example, it has been estimated that 50 percent of our drugs and pharmaceuticals have been developed since 1950, and that over 80 percent of the agricultural chemicals in use in the early 1960's were not available in the same form during World War II. This flood of new products has contributed to the increasingly competitive nature of many industries. In brief:

> The pattern of development of the chemical industry reflects the impact of competition on the technological front. Research and development is designed to develop new products, to improve old products, and to seek new uses for products. One result has been that the products of the chemical industry are among those with the highest growth rates. The extensive interindustry and interproduct competition . . . testify to the effectiveness of these research efforts which have added a significant dimension to competition in this industry.[1]

It should also be emphasized that the tempo of change is quickening, not slowing down. As Paul B. Wishart, the chairman of Honeywell, Inc., has emphasized, we can expect "giant technological strides through research

---

[1] Backman, Jules, *Competition in the Chemical Industry,* Manufacturing Chemists' Association, Inc., Washington, D.C., 1964, p. 46.

and development, overcoming existing products through superior performance and solutions employing entirely new concepts." The result will be "entirely new products and solutions to consumer needs." [2] The increasing availability of substitute products is a vital economic fact of life in American industry. The competitive implications for existing products must constantly be kept in mind by management.

PRICE COMPETITION

Competition reflects and involves an inseparable bundle of forces and pressures of which prices are a vital part. However, price changes do not represent the entire competitive picture. Price competition should not be treated separately or in isolation from the other competitive forces which are concurrently experienced in business.

Price competition has become increasingly vigorous in many industries. The prices of many chemicals, paper products, aluminum products, computers, and electrical equipment and appliances were buffeted badly in the early 1960's.

Oligopoly theory emphasizes the manner in which companies in industries characterized by relatively few sellers tend to consider the reactions of their competitors to any actions they may take in such areas as price and output. Each seller considers the effects of its own output and price decisions on those of its competitors and the probable retaliatory actions of those competitors. The underlying assumption is that the largest concern is so big that its decisions determine the price.

According to oligopoly theory it is difficult, therefore, for a concern to obtain some of the business of its rivals by lowering price. Slogans such as "Live and let live" as well as "Don't spoil the market" are considered to be characteristic of oligopolistic situations. Such a situation is presumed to inhibit price competition.

But it is clear that there are oligopolists and oligopolists. The fact of oligopoly does not of itself assure any specific price behavior or competitive pattern. As S. C. Oppenheim has observed: ". . . oligopoly competition may be as virile as competition in an industry with a large number of small or medium-sized firms." [3]

---

[2] *Nation's Business*, August 1963, p. 62.

[3] Oppenheim, S. Chesterfield, "The Sherman Act and Internal Company Growth," in *Antitrust in an Expanding Economy*, National Industrial Conference Board, 1962, p. 11.

Each of the five oligopolistic industries cited earlier for increasingly vigorous competition has experienced above-average growth in the past quarter of a century. Hence they account for an increasing proportion of total manufacturing activity:

	Percent of Value Added in All Manufacturing		
	1939	*1947*	*1964*
Electrical machinery	3.8	5.2	8.7
Paper and paper products	3.6	3.9	3.8
Chemicals and allied products	6.9	6.6	9.3
Aluminum products (rolling and primary drawing)	0.3	0.3	0.6
Office equipment computers	0.3	0.3	0.6
	14.9	16.3	23.0

It certainly is significant that the five industries listed account for 23.0 percent of the value added by manufacture and that the proportion has been increasing steadily. Not every item produced by these industries has been subject to vigorous price competition. Nor should it be inferred that price competition is limited only to these industries, nor that the remainder of the manufacturing economy has no price competition, nor that price changes alone show the presence of vigorous competition. These industries are cited primarily as outstanding illustrations of invigorated price competition.

The pressure on prices in these areas has reflected: (*a*) new entrants into the market (for example, computers and organic chemicals), (*b*) the price-cutting proclivities of smaller companies (aluminum-fabricated products), (*c*) the search for volume by large companies (paper and electrical equipment), (*d*) the development of substitute products with the accompanying expansion of the scope of the market (plastics), and (*e*) periodic excess capacity as marked growth in plant capacity temporarily outstrips demand (chemicals).

PRICE LEADERSHIP

Additional evidence of the invigoration of price competition is found in the unwillingness of many companies to follow all price increases inaugurated by their competitors. Price leadership, particularly in oligopolistic industries, has often been cited as evidence of lack of price competition.

Some writers have gone so far as to describe price leadership and price followership as a "form of tacit collusion."[4] However, as Corwin Edwards has recognized: "Price leadership differs from tacit collusion . . . [because] there may be no interchange of opinion, even on an informal basis, prior to an announcement of the leader's policy."[5]

Price leadership is found in most sectors of American industry. It is particularly important in industries whose products are standardized or are considered to be completely substitutable for each other. Under such conditions, it is claimed, each firm recognizes the probability that price cuts will be met by rivals and that there is danger of retaliatory price reductions.

When a company wishes to change its price, it must consider whether rivals will match the change. In this situation, a company generally will be reluctant to raise or to lower prices in the absence of a major change in the economic conditions affecting that product. The change may be a significant rise in labor costs, changes in raw material costs, large increases or decreases in demand, the development of substitute products, or other developments that have an impact on the industry. Whatever the reason, it is usually the judgment of the price leader that determines the timing and magnitude of the price change. In effect, the price leader acts as a *barometer*. Increases reflect the price leader's response to basic economic pressures.

Price leaders were closely followed by other companies throughout the inflationary decade after the end of World War II. However, *it should be emphasized that the general tendency for many companies to follow practically all price increases in the earlier postwar years did not reflect "tacit collusion" as has been suggested. Rather, it reflected to a large extent the inflationary environment in which those patterns emerged.* Under conditions of inflation, strong pressures push up prices, wages, and profits. Often the blame for the price rise is directed at one group. This is reflected in the claims by industry that higher prices are the result of higher labor costs and the claims by labor that higher prices result from the desire for higher profits. Such claims ignore the fact that the fundamental pressures for higher prices, higher wages, and profits are generated by fiscal or monetary

---

[4] Stigler, George J., *The Theory of Price*, The Macmillan Company, 1952, p. 234.

[5] Edwards, Corwin D., *Maintaining Competition*, McGraw-Hill Book Company, New York, 1949, p. 36.

inflation. Actually, the reason for prompt price followership by practically all firms is to be found in these inflationary pressures.

In the early 1960's, however, as competitive pressures expanded, in a number of instances there developed an unwillingness by companies to follow increases initiated by a former price leader. The weakening of price leadership as compared with the early postwar practices reflected the reduction in inflationary pressures and the new competitive influences that were developing. For many products, announced price increases had to be reversed within a fairly short period of time.[6]

Both large and small companies have been rebuffed in their efforts to raise prices. The large number of reversals reflects the changing economic environment and the increasing competitive pressures. The fact that smaller companies attempted to lead prices upward in some instances probably reflected the profit squeeze they were experiencing.

There also has been some breakdown in the traditional leadership pattern. Companies which were primarily followers have been acting as price leaders more frequently, as the experience in the aluminum and steel[7] industries demonstrates.

Similarly, the failure of smaller companies to follow price increases initiated by the large producers reflected increasing emphasis on price competition.

PRICE SHADING

Another indication of the intensification of price competition is found in the growing tendency to shade list prices. Often such price concessions have been initiated by smaller companies. In order to remain competitive, the big companies then have had to lower their prices to the new level established. The widespread nature of this practice is indicated by the diversity of products that have been affected. In the early and mid-1960's the list included circuit breakers, ethylene, paper bags, power transformers, polybutadiene synthetic rubber, cement, propane gas, phthalic anhydride, copper

---

[6] For a list of 43 instances in which price increases were not followed and had to be reversed in the 1961–1964 period, see the author's testimony in the *Hearings on Economic Concentration* before the Senate Subcommittee on Antitrust and Monopoly, Committee on the Judiciary, Washington, D.C., March 1965, Part 2, pp. 570, 890–896.

[7] In 1958, Armco led the upward movement of prices, thus displacing U.S. Steel, which traditionally had been the price leader. See Weiss, Leonard V., *Economics and American Industry,* John Wiley & Sons, Inc., 1961, pp. 293–295.

water tubes, aluminum siding, and stainless steel. Important industry leaders, including Kennecott Copper, General Electric, International Paper, Alpha Portland Cement, Union Carbide, and Alcoa, had to follow price shading initiated by smaller firms.

Clearly, these developments reflect a new dimension to price competition in many sectors of the economy. Large producers are not free to raise prices arbitrarily without relationship to economic pressures merely because there are only a few companies in a market. Nor are they able to avoid price declines. *There often is a considerable difference between the apparent power inherent in an oligopolistic industry and the ability to exercise that power.* These competitive pressures have become one of the most important determinants of effective pricing. The economic environment provides tremendous constraints upon pricing that are not accounted for by critics such as J. Kenneth Galbraith.[8]

NONPRICE COMPETITION

Companies compete increasingly in such areas as research, quality, credit terms, technical services, brand names, and advertising.[9] This type of competition—*nonprice* competition—has been of major importance throughout American industry. An interesting illustration is found in the more liberal warranties given with new automobiles. Under the pressure of competition, these warranties reached 50,000 miles—or five years. But they became so costly that in 1967 their scope had to be reduced.

Charles C. Mortimer, chairman of General Foods, has succinctly summarized the role of nonprice competition by noting that what keeps executives awake nights "is the specter of some competitor—big or little—coming out with a really significant improvement in his product or service, a super-duper new model, a glamorous new style, a package improvement that captivates the consumer, a patentable feature that gives him a basic advantage, a new advertising or promotion appeal that really wows the consumers."[10] Such a competitive environment keeps businessmen on their toes and compels them to seek out new products and better ways of producing older ones.

---

[8] Galbraith, J. K., *The New Industrial State*, Houghton Mifflin Company, 1967.
[9] Backman, Jules, *Advertising and Competition*, New York University Press, 1967.
[10] *Nation's Business*, August 1963, p. 60.

FOREIGN COMPETITION: THE INTERNATIONALIZATION OF BUSINESS

The dramatic shift in foreign trade in steel, with imports rising steadily; the significant impact of Japanese competition in textiles, transistors, and other products; and the increase in the sale of foreign cars all illustrate the growing influence of foreign competition in American markets. These pressures from abroad will intensify and will spread to additional products. The devaluation of the British pound late in 1967 was accompanied by a reduction in prices for some British products in world trade with an accompanying improvement in their competitive position.

Western Europe and Japan have expanded their productive capacity substantially in the past decade. Much of this capacity is new and embodies the latest technological developments. It also represents capacity which is in excess of their domestic needs. The result is a highly productive plant which, when combined with much lower labor costs, has made it possible for foreign producers at times to undersell our domestic concerns. As a consequence, an increasing number of products have flowed into American markets and have invigorated competition. Similarly, competition has been increased in third markets.

Developments such as the St. Lawrence Seaway, with the accompanying lower transportation costs, are playing a role. Tariffs have been reduced very substantially. And the consummation of the Kennedy round of tariff reductions means that additional imports will be competitive in the American market.

The growth of the Common Market also is of great significance. The development of a new free trade area, almost as large in population as the United States, already is having an important effect upon industries in those countries. There has been an appreciable increase in the size of new plants so that they are benefiting from the economies of mass production. The competitive effects of this development remain to be fully realized. However, as already is clear, one result will be more vigorous competition in this country.

Many companies throughout the world are rapidly becoming internationalized. American companies have been investing heavily abroad while, to a lesser extent, foreign companies have been investing here. This internationalization of industry should continue in the absence of government action such as the restrictions on new overseas investments announced by President Johnson early in 1968. It should broaden the size of geographic markets and increase competition from and among overseas companies, thus adding yet another new dimension to competition.

Public Information on Pricing

One of the important changes in industry has been the increasing flow of public information concerning pricing practices and policies since World War II. Prior to that conflict, pricing was an area shrouded in almost complete secrecy. The general philosophy was that it was no one's business how prices were set; hence little or no information was made available voluntarily.

The scanty information available was widely scattered and difficult to assemble. The curtain was lifted on occasion by a Federal Trade Commission study (for example, that on chain-store pricing around 1930), by Congressional hearings (those dealing with basing-point pricing), and by scattered articles.[11] In addition, the reports written about experience with the National Recovery Administration contain some descriptions of pricing practices.[12] The Temporary National Economic Committee just prior to World War II developed several valuable studies in this area.[13]

During World War II, the Federal Government embarked upon the most intensive and comprehensive program of price fixing in our history. From 1941 to 1946, price increases had to be justified before government officials (often economists recruited from the universities), whose main role was to say no. Increasingly businessmen had to examine the procedures they used in setting prices and the factors to which they gave weight. One result was a greater understanding of the pricing process. The experience during the Korean conflict acted to reinforce this understanding.

Even more important was the ever widening sector of industry that be-

---

[11] Probably the most comprehensive review of price policy for a leading corporation is Donaldson Brown's analysis of General Motors pricing policy, which appeared in a little-known publication. See Brown, Donaldson, "Pricing Policy in Relation to Financial Control," *Management and Administration*, February 1924, pp. 195–98; March 1924, pp. 283–86; and April 1924, pp. 417–22. The highlights of these articles are reproduced in Backman, Jules, *Price Practices and Price Policies*, Ronald Press, 1953, pp. 359–365.

[12] See, for example, Thorp, Willard L., and A. N. Caesar, "A Study of Open Filing in the Electrical Manufacturing Industry," *Work Materials No. 78*, National Recovery Administration, Division of Review, March 1936.

[13] See, for example, Nelson, Saul, and Walter G. Keim, "Price Behavior and Business Policy," *TNEC Monograph No. 1*, Temporary National Economic Committee, 1940, and "Industrial Wage Rates, Labor Costs, and Price Policies," *TNEC Monograph No. 5*, 1940.

came concerned with its public image, particularly during the period of postwar price inflation. More and more often, companies issued public statements designed to explain (rationalize) their hikes in prices. A greater willingness developed to describe pricing practices in annual reports as well as in speeches by company officials. Greater cooperation also was extended to scholars in their efforts to understand industrial pricing. Probably the most comprehensive effort in this direction was the study of 20 large companies by A. D. H. Kaplan and his colleagues at The Brookings Institution.[14]

These voluntary dispensations of information about pricing were supplemented by a number of Congressional hearings. Of particular interest were the Kefauver Committee's hearings on administered prices, which extended over 29 volumes and contained considerable testimony concerning the pricing of steel, automobiles, drugs, electrical equipment, asphalt roofing, and bread. These hearings also covered such areas as prenotification of price increases and competitive bidding. Moreover, hearings in other areas, like tariffs, began to contain a considerable amount of pricing information as competitive pressures affecting prices were created by the expanding flow of imports: steel, carpets, cotton textiles, glass, radios, toys, and so on.

Finally, an increasing number of antitrust cases involving price fixing shed additional light on pricing practices. Easily the outstanding illustration was provided by the Philadelphia antitrust cases in the electrical machinery industry.[15] The widespread publicity attending these cases and the jail terms imposed on several corporate officials sent shock waves through American industry.

The growing number of Robinson-Patman Act cases also has contributed to the public's greater awareness of pricing procedures. The Great Atlantic and Pacific Tea Company and Standard Oil of Indiana cases are two leading examples.

The combination of Congressional hearings, antitrust cases, wage-price

---

[14] Kaplan, A. D. H., Joel B. Dirlam, and Robert F. Lanzillotti, *Pricing in Big Business,* The Brookings Institution, 1958. See also Backman, Jules, *The Economics of the Electrical Machinery Industry,* New York University Press, 1962, Ch. V, and *Chemical Prices, Productivity, Wages, and Profits,* Manufacturing Chemists' Association, Inc., Washington, D.C., November 1964, Ch. I. For pricing statements covering many companies see Backman, Jules, *Pricing: Policies and Practices,* National Industrial Conference Board, 1961.

[15] See Smith, Richard Austin, "The Incredible Electrical Conspiracy," *Fortune,* April 1961, pp. 132–137, 170–180, and May 1961, pp. 161–164, 210–224; and *Price Fixing and Bid Rigging in the Electrical Manufacturing Industry,* Senate Subcommittee on Antitrust and Monopoly (Kefauver Committee), Parts 27 and 28, April and May 1961.

guidelines, and increasing concern with public image has brought the public relations aspect of pricing to the fore. As Kaplan and his associates have pointed out: ". . . companies in the limelight [desire] to be respectable in the eyes of the public and their business associates."[16] It is impossible to quantify the importance of this factor, but it undoubtedly affects the thinking of top management today to an extent which would have been considered inconceivable before World War II. It has resulted in, among other things, an expanded flow of explanations of price actions by leading corporations.

Expanding Role of Government

With rare exceptions, pricing was considered to be entirely within the province of the private economy during periods of peace prior to World War II. Government control of prices was significant during World War I and covered practically all products during World War II and during the Korean conflict. Since the end of World War II, the Federal Government has been increasingly concerned about prices set in the private economy. While it has not resorted to direct price fixing (except in connection with milk and other agricultural products), the Federal Government has affected the pricing process by criticizing price increases publicly and privately.

Illustrations of government interest in this country include the experience of the steel industry in the postwar years and the operation of the wage-price guidelines in the middle 1960's; British concern is illustrated by the price cuts suggested in 1966 for soaps and detergents.[17]

POSTWAR STEEL PRICES

Throughout the post-World War II period, considerable political pressure was generated whenever steel-price increases were announced. The reaction in each case was based on the purported unique position of steel in

---

[16] Kaplan *et al., op. cit.,* p. 269.

[17] The British Monopolies Commission recommended that promotional costs for soaps and detergents be cut by 40 percent and prices by 20 percent. (See Monopolies Commission, *Household Detergents,* Her Majesty's Stationery Office, London, August 3, 1966, pp. 41–42, 44–45.) The British producers resisted the recommendation of the Monopolies Commission, and the issue was finally resolved by the two leading producers, each agreeing to introduce three brands which would sell at lower prices than existing brands and for which promotional costs would be kept relatively low.

the American economy. However, although steel was a bellwether in the past, this is no longer true.

The direct and indirect consequences of steel-price increases have been considerably exaggerated. Thus, for example, President Harry Truman stated in 1947 that steel-price increases "would be a serious blow to our economy." [18] In the late 1940's, steel-price increases also were criticized by the Council of Economic Advisers and in Congressional hearings.[19] Senator Estes Kefauver led the criticism in the late 1950's and started the hearings on administered prices with the steel industry.[20]

The issue of government intervention in steel pricing came to a head in the spring of 1962 when U.S. Steel Corporation raised its prices by an average of $6 per ton, or about 3.5 percent, and President Kennedy led a determined assault to have these price increases rescinded. He described them as a "wholly unjustifiable and irresponsible defiance of the public interest." After several days of great political pressure, several steel companies (Inland Steel, Armco, and Kaiser Steel) refused to follow the increases posted by the other leading steel companies, and the increases were rescinded.

In the interim it was reported that four antitrust investigations were conceived, the Department of Defense began to divert purchases away from U.S. Steel, legislation to roll back steel prices was proposed, and Congressional committees scheduled hearings to study the price increase.[21]

The lesson of this experience was quickly drawn both by steel-industry officials and by those in other industries. General price increases in highly visible industries such as steel were to be under continuous scrutiny. The reactions of top government officials to any across-the-board price increases became one of the important ingredients of price making in important sectors of the American economy. After 1962, steel-price changes were limited to groups of products rather than applied across the board as had generally been the case in the earlier postwar adjustments—and the magnitudes

---

[18] *The New York Times,* July 15, 1947.

[19] *Hearing on Increases in Steel Prices* before the Joint Committee on the Economic Report, 80th Congress, 2nd Session, Washington, D.C., March 1948, and *December 1949 Steel Price Increases,* 81st Congress, 2nd Session, Washington, D.C., January 1950; and Subcommittee on Study of Monopoly Power of the House Judiciary Committee, *Study of Monopoly Power-Steel,* Parts 4A and 4B, 81st Congress, 2nd Session, Washington, D.C., 1950.

[20] See *Hearings on Administered Prices* before the Subcommittee on Antitrust and Monopoly, Committee on the Judiciary, United States Senate, 1957, Parts 2 to 4; and Report of the Committee, *Administered Prices, Steel,* Senate Report No. 1387, 1958.

[21] *The New York Times,* April 23, 1962.

of such increases probably were smaller than would have been the case in the absence of the 1962 confrontation.

THE WAGE-PRICE GUIDELINES

The wage-price guidelines were designed to restrict labor-cost increases and to maintain a relatively stable price level. During 1965 and 1966, the Council of Economic Advisers and the Secretary of Defense, as well as the President of the United States, actively intervened to prevent announced higher prices from becoming effective for a number of products, including aluminum, copper, cigarettes, and molybdenum.

Aluminum. Prices of aluminum ingot and fabricated products were increased by half a cent and one cent respectively in November 1965. The National Administration threatened to dump substantial amounts of stockpiled aluminum on the market if the increase remained in effect. Within ten days the producers rescinded the announced rise.[22]

Copper. On November 1, 1965, a small producer, Copper Range Company, increased the price of copper by two cents a pound. Other copper companies, with the sole exception of Kennecott, matched this higher price. The Federal Government, through Defense Secretary McNamara, announced a program to reduce prices and to increase domestic supplies of copper. The program included the sale of 200,000 tons of stockpiled copper. As a result of these actions, the price increase was canceled by all the copper producers.[23]

Cigarettes. In March 1966, American Tobacco increased wholesale cigarette prices. The major cigarette companies immediately raised their prices. However, R. J. Reynolds withdrew its price advance at the request of President Johnson. A week after the initial price hike, American Tobacco halved it. Soon thereafter, all the companies with the exception of R. J. Reynolds followed suit. It was not until early May that Reynolds matched the higher prices.[24]

Molybdenum. In July 1966, American Metal Climax and Molybdenum Corporation of America announced a 5 percent price increase on molybdenum products. Gardner Ackley, chairman of the Council of Economic

---

[22] *The Wall Street Journal,* December 7, 1966.
[23] *Op. cit.,* November 30, 1965.
[24] *Op. cit.,* June 2, 1967.

Advisers, was sharply critical of the advance. As a result of heavy pressure by the Johnson Administration, the higher prices were canceled.[25]

In addition to these public actions, officials intervened in many situations privately. During the year 1966, the CEA reported that it

> . . . became involved in regard to perhaps 50 product lines for which price increases were either imminent or had been announced by one or more firms. In the typical case, the Council learned in one way or another of a price increase that was contemplated or that had been announced by one or more producers. In some instances, companies contemplating price changes themselves brought the subject to the Council's attention. Where the Council learned of an important actual or impending price increase, its procedure was to send letters or telegrams to all principal producers of the product. In urgent cases, telephone calls substituted for letters or telegrams. If some firms had already announced price increases, they were asked to reconsider. Those who had not so announced were asked to avoid them if possible. In all cases, an invitation was extended to meet with the Council to discuss the matter.

> In the private discussions which often followed these communications, the companies explained the reasons why a price increase was considered appropriate, and the Government representatives presented any information available to them which appeared relevant to the price decision.

> The Council . . . explains the public interest in price stability, and the company is urged to take this interest fully into account in making its decision. These meetings are ordinarily not reported publicly unless revealed by the company involved.[26]

What was the effect of this governmental intervention? The CEA reported:

> The outcome of these activities cannot be fully known. In a number of cases, it is clear that price increases which were announced or contemplated have been rescinded, reduced in amount or coverage, or delayed. *Some companies have indicated that their subsequent price decisions were affected* even where their decision in the immediate case was not changed.

> . . . Almost invariably the companies involved have recognized a larger public interest in their pricing decisions and have made a sincere effort to take that interest into account. Some large companies agreed to give

---

[25] *Op. cit.*, January 11, 1967.
[26] *Economic Report of the President,* January 1967, p. 126.

the Council advance notice of their intention to change prices.[27] [Italics added.]

At least one individual can report from personal experience that some companies gave very careful consideration to the probable reaction of government officials as one important factor when they were contemplating price increases during this period.

✦   ✦   ✦

Government is certain to play an increasing role in private pricing decisions. This is the trend throughout the world. Wage-price guidelines—or "income policy," the term often used abroad—provide "yardsticks" to determine the "reasonableness" of prices in many countries. The fact that meaningful objective yardsticks of price reasonableness are not available (nor is it probable that they will be created) means that subjective standards must be used. Inevitably, this approach for the most part finds price increases objectionable, particularly during periods of price inflation. At such times, governments are unwilling to deal with the real causes of price inflation—which are found in unbalanced federal budgets, excessive creation of money and credit, and increases in labor costs which far exceed gains in output per man-hour. However, it is politically more attractive to attempt to influence prices which are the result, rather than inflation which is the cause, of higher prices.

---

27 *Ibid.*, p. 127.

Index